Wicked Crescenta Valley

Gary Keyes and Mike Lawler

The History Press

Published by The History Press
Charleston, SC 29403
www.historypress.net

First published 2014

Manufactured in the United States

ISBN 978.1.62619.306.2

Library of Congress CIP data applied for.

Contents

Introduction

This book is a companion to our first book, *Murder and Mayhem in the Crescenta Valley*. With these books being released back to back, one might think that the Crescenta Valley is a terrible place to live. It isn't—in fact, it's better than most places. The truth is that any community could easily spawn several local history books of similar evil nature. Most communities choose not to. Most communities want to see only the good sides of their histories. But not the Crescenta Valley. Our history is so dynamic and colorful that to only cover the "good" aspects would not do it justice.

Admittedly, we have always been attracted to the darker side of history. Perhaps it's the idea that these portions of history are often hidden away, and so discovering them is like finding out a lost family secret. It could be that studying the dark side of our history is just more challenging. Finding the "good" portions of history is easy—finding the "bad" portions takes some detective work. Perhaps it's that it humanizes those larger-than-life historic characters of which we have made heroes. More likely, however, it's just that it realistically levels the playing field between the sanctified "good old days" and the often demonized world of today. It is our opinion that the world is not a worse place today. Human nature—which can be marked by greed, prejudice and jealousy—is the same as it's always been. The outcome of those natural impulses—crime, injustice and violence—is simply better documented in the modern world. The world isn't going to hell in a handbasket. The basket is right where it always has been—somewhere between heaven and hell. We simply have a clearer view of it today.

And so take this admittedly discouraging look at our valley and balance these heinous tales with the good stories of our history that you have probably read in the many books already written. If you can keep the two sides balanced in your mind, you will end up with a fairly accurate feel for the history of the Crescenta Valley. Our valley is simply a colorful place in the world where both noble and flawed humans, with all their good and bad traits and impulses, have made their marks on history.

Chapter 1
Sex

The Dance Wars

In the 1890s, fights broke out between two groups of students at the La Cañada School when one group began using the school for Saturday night dances. Other students felt that the dancing was immoral, especially the waltz. The problem was further complicated by the fact that the school also housed the only church in La Cañada. The dances were chaperoned by a new and attractive teacher, Ms. Mamie Sexton. The church group did not like the appearance of the students leaving the dances; perhaps they were having too much fun. When several boys admitted that they attended the dances only to watch Ms. Sexton dance, the fat was in the fire.

The religious forces denounced this jezebel who was corrupting the young men of the village. The town was divided between pro-dance and anti-dance, pro-Sexton and anti-Sexton partisans. To resolve the issue, an election was held. The leader of the anti-dance group was Jessie Knight, the largest employer in the valley. He called his side of the dispute the "Forces of Righteousness." On the day of the election, tensions ran high. One pro-dance student horsewhipped an anti-dancer for claiming that he was courting Ms. Sexton. Knight posted armed guards at the polling site to ensure that God's will be done. The anti-dancers were winning the election;

La Cañada Elementary School in the late 1800s—ground zero for the city's "dance wars." This site today is Memorial Park at Foothill and La Cañada Boulevards. *Glendale Public Library*.

however, at the last minute, rancher Tom McClellan, or "T-Mac," as he was known, brought his Mexican ranch hands to vote pro-dancing. The pro-dancers won the election, and the anti-dancing forces were crushed, but they did not take it lying down. Knight formed a private school on his own ranch that was attended by half of La Cañada students. The public school no longer had enough students to function properly. T-Mac then enrolled the sons and daughters of his ranch hands. The feud continued for another two years, at which point Knight was elected to the school board. His first order of business was to fire Ms. Sexton. The new schoolmaster, E.L. French, healed the breach. He proposed a separate church building and dance hall. The real question was why no one had thought of this seemingly obvious solution two years before.

Thanks go out to John Newcombe for this material, which was taken from his award-winning film *Rancho La Cañada: Then and Now*.

The Nudist Camp in La Tuna Canyon

Dating back to the 1930s, one of the first nudist camps in the United States had its home close to Crescenta Valley, just over the Verdugo Mountains in La Tuna Canyon. In 1934, two pioneers in the phenomenon of social nudism, Hobart and Lura Glassey, established one of the first U.S. nudist camps in Orange County near Lake Elsinore. It was a business, with paying members granted access to a private campground. The Glasseys had quick success, particularly after a widely circulated movie about nudism was filmed there. In 1935, when Lura became pregnant, they opted to move closer to medical facilities and purchased land in La Tuna Canyon for a new nudist camp.

The new facility, Fraternity Elysia, was located at 9804 La Tuna Canyon Road in a little canyon on the south side of the road. Today, that small canyon is the site of a newer housing development at the intersection of La Tuna Canyon and Morning Glow Roads. The camp was a hit, and this new nudist colony was once again the setting for a nudist movie, 1938's *The Unashamed*, which enjoyed a wide theater showing. A famous member of Fraternity Elysia was Caltech seismologist Charles Richter, namesake of the Richter scale, which we use to measure earthquakes. He and his wife were members of Fraternity Elysia from its beginnings in 1935, the same year that the Richter scale became the standard measure of earthquake intensity.

Although the camp was wildly successful, tragedy seemed to follow Fraternity Elysia. Hobart Glassey died tragically at Elysia in 1938 in a fall that broke his neck. In 1939, actress Dawn Hope Noel, daughter of then famous film and stage actress Adele Blood, committed suicide at Elysia. This supposed evidence of the "corruption of mind" caused by nudism created a storm of negative publicity for the camp and for nudism in general.

By 1940, local authorities had decided that Fraternity Elysia was a liability to the morals of Los Angeles, and they began a series of raids on the camp. The now widowed Lura Glassey was arrested numerous times before World War II on oddball charges such as "allowing men and women to mingle while nude." The camp, which had no neighbors and thus no one to offend, was staked out by officers, who would observe it through binoculars and even produced a two-minute film to show in court. The film was taken through a telephoto lens from surrounding hillsides and showed men, women and children sunbathing nude and semi-nude around a swimming pool. The charges never amounted to more than fines and probation, as World War II gave the police more important things to do.

When the war ended, the LAPD could once more focus on Fraternity Elysia. The arrest that spelled the end of the camp took place in 1946. Two members of the department's vice squad, a male and female officer, posed as nudists and applied for membership to the camp. On a tour of the camp, they observed "a score of persons including 2 young girls and 4 boys" playing badminton, ping-pong and sunbathing in the nude at the camp. When two more officers showed up, someone yelled, "The coppers are here!" and everyone quickly put their clothes back on. However, Lura Glassey and her new business partner, Henry Broening, were arrested and charged with violating the city's new anti-nudity ordinance. They were convicted in a jury trial and sentenced to several months in jail. Broening chose to serve his sentence and be done with it, but Lura Glassey appealed the verdict.

With the help of the American Civil Liberties Union, Glassey appealed to the Supreme Court in 1947, arguing that "nudism is a social belief, and not legally limited unless there is a danger to society." But the court ruled that "the appellants had not demonstrated that the ordinance unduly restricted personal liberties." The original conviction stood. Lura Glassy went to jail, and the nudist camp in La Tuna Canyon closed and became an interesting side note of our local lore.

Inga Arvad

Inga Arvad led an extremely interesting life. In the early 1930s, she was crowned Miss Europe in a beauty contest. She accepted the crown from famous French actor Maurice Chevalier. At seventeen, she married Egyptian aristocrat Kamil Abel Nabi. After divorcing Nabi, she later appeared in two Danish films and married her director, Paul Fejos. Arvad eventually moved into journalism and met Herman Goring and Joseph Goebbels. Goring was quite taken with her and invited her to his wedding, where he introduced her to his best man, Adolf Hitler. Hitler described the honey blonde as "the perfect Nordic beauty." Arvad went on to interview Hitler on two or three occasions. She attended the 1936 Olympics with Hitler and, according to an FBI report, slept with the Fuehrer. Writing about her meeting with Hitler, she said, "You immediately like him. He seems lonely. The eyes, showing a kind heart, stare right at you. They sparkle with force."

Inga came to the attention of the FBI when authorities believed that she had become the mistress of Swedish industrialist Axel Wenner-Gren. Wenner-Gren was the world's wealthiest man. He was the owner of the Bofors Armaments Factory, founder of the Electrolux Vacuum Cleaner Company and owner of Paradise Island in the Bahamas. The FBI suspected him of using his 320-foot yacht to refuel German U-boats. No proof of a relationship between Wenner-Gren and Arvad has been found.

Arvad came to the United States in 1941 to continue her journalistic career. The FBI suspected her as a German spy and continued its surveillance. One night in November of that year, a young FBI agent was embarrassed to be assigned to the recording of Inga's love tryst with a young naval officer. The agent was shocked to recognize the voice of a former Harvard classmate, John F. Kennedy. The FBI bugged the couples' love nest and taped them making love on more than one occasion. Kennedy later boasted that when he got to Washington, he would retrieve the tapes, but he never did. Kennedy wanted to fire J. Edgar Hoover, director of the FBI, but he never did. The compromising tapes were one of Hoover's methods of insuring his job. The affair threatened to derail JFK's naval career, as the office of U.S. Naval Intelligence wanted to discharge him. Instead, because of political pressure, he was assigned to the backwaters of Charleston, South Carolina. If the navy thought this transfer would end Kennedy's affair, they were to be disappointed. According to Nigel Cawthorne, John Kennedy wanted to marry Inga. Joseph Kennedy, John's father, objected to this plan. He pointed out that Inga was still married and was not Catholic. But these objections did not stop Joseph from trying to seduce her himself. He was in his seventies at the time. Eventually, the FBI's JFK/Arvad file would grow to 628 pages.

Inga continued her amazing career by becoming engaged to Robert Boothby, a member of the English Parliament, in May 1945. He met Inga in Los Angeles while attending a conference. Boothby sent her a twenty-page letter pleading with her to marry him. Inga accepted but, fearing the effect her past would have on Boothby's career, later broke off the engagement. In 1946, Inga briefly renewed her relationship with JFK. The last meeting between the two took place in November of that year. This was three months before she married cowboy star Tim McCoy, thirty years her senior. Six months later, their son, Ronald, was born. Years later, Inga told Ronald that she was pregnant at the time of her marriage and did not know whether his father was McCoy or JFK. After this fascinating life, Inga retired and lived in seclusion in La Cañada Flintridge on Dalridge Road.

This material comes from *Sex Lives of the Presidents* by Nigel Cawthorne and *The Dark Side of Camelot* by Seymour Hersh. The most complete account is to be found in *J. Edgar Hoover* by Curt Gentry.

Prostitution

The foothill communities were a happening place in the 1920s—the era of flappers and coonskin coats. The Crescenta Valley with its canyons, gullies and caves was a perfect fit for the production and storage of moonshine during Prohibition. What is now the Pacific Design Center on Foothill Boulevard was a rumored storage site for moonshine. Ford's Inn, located in Whiting Woods, was a favored location for the consumption of illegal alcohol. Along with illegal booze, prostitution was booming. Our area has a long affiliation with the oldest profession in the world.

Perry Whiting purchased 44 acres of mountain land in the mid-1920s. Later purchases of 446 acres and 260 acres rounded out his holdings. This area today is, of course, Whiting Woods. All but 10 acres of this land was too steep for practical use. The Pasadena Mountain Club was established on these 10 acres. The club was owned by four or five stockholders, and gentlemen could join for fifty cents. The club consisted of a small house and ten small one-room cabins. The cabins were rented out and used for prostitution. The district attorney closed the club under the Red Light Abatement Act.

In the 1960s, Dr. William Thomas, then principal of Crescenta Valley High School, related to his faculty a personal experience. It was Christmas, and he and the Key Club were distributing Christmas baskets to the less fortunate. He stumbled upon a local house of ill repute. It was located above the Cuesta Theater on Colorado Boulevard in Glendale. He said the students did not realize where they were, but he did!

In the 1970s, a prostitution bust was made in La Crescenta. The police made an arrangement for services by placing a call to the woman from the Safeway on Foothill Boulevard. The woman and her husband operated from an apartment on Altura Avenue. It turned out that the husband, a teacher in La Cañada, was pimping out his wife.

A forty-two-year-old woman was arrested in 2006 on suspicion of prostitution on the 2900 block of Honolulu Avenue. The site was an

A zoomed-in view of this 1915 landscape photo of the Verdugo Mountains reveals a clear view of the Pasadena Mountain Club, a bar and whorehouse located in the canyon where the beautiful community of Whiting Woods is today. Visible is the main house where drinks were served and, behind that, the ten shacks where the prostitutes plied their trade. *Glendale Public Library.*

unmarked office that was being advertised as a massage clinic. This had been the sixth prostitution arrest in La Crescenta and Montrose that year.

In August 2011, Xianoyan Zhao was arrested in Montrose by undercover police officers for offering sex in exchange for money. Her clinic was listed as "S.L. Acc-Care." Two other sites, "Acupuncture" and "Integrated Pain Clinic," were also raided. Charged with prostitution were Feng En Lu (fifty-six), Li Juan Sun (forty-eight), Oing Ang (forty-six), Mei Ling Yu (forty-six) and Hui Yung Liang (thirty-seven).

PERVERSION, CHILD ABUSE AND OTHER SEX CRIMES

Gus Meins

Gus Meins was born March 6, 1893, and died on August 1, 1940, in La Crescenta. Meins was a famous film director who had come to the United States from Frankfurt, Germany, in the early 1900s. He started his career as a cartoonist for the *Los Angeles Evening Herald*. In 1919, he became a gag writer for Mack Sennett, an innovator of slapstick comedy. Meins's film career

Gus Meins was a top Hollywood director in the 1920s and '30s, with the classic Laurel and Hardy film *Babes in Toyland* to his credit. He was known for his knack for directing children and was the principal director for the *Our Gang* comedies. In 1940, Meins was charged with molesting boys and committed suicide in La Crescenta. Here he's pictured during happier days with his *Our Gang* stars. *www.benny-drinnon.blogspot.com.*

continued to grow. He became a director and worked with Stan Laurel and Oliver Hardy in the classic film *Babes in Toyland*, better known as *The March of the Wooden Soldiers*. The film was praised for its comedic timing and for the monkey that played a bastardized Mickey Mouse. Meins also directed *Mama's Little Pirate*, *Sprucing Up* and *Lucky Corner*. He worked with Hal Roach in directing the *Our Gang* comedies from 1934 to 1936. He also directed the Buster Brown serials and is credited with over 160 short films. The legendary actors with whom he worked include Thelma Todd, Zasu Pitts and Charlie Chase. Meins was known as one of the kindest men in Hollywood and had a special knack for directing child performers. However, his affinity for child actors led to accusations of child molestation. On August 1 1940, Meins was arrested for molesting six boys between the ages of ten and fifteen. He swore that he was innocent but told his wife that the charges would destroy him even if he were found innocent. He told his son, "You probably won't see me again." The day he was released on bail, he drove to a Montrose suburb and committed suicide via carbon monoxide poisoning. He was survived by his wife and son, Douglas Meins.

Richard Allen Henry

Richard Henry was the associate pastor at Holy Redeemer Catholic Church in Montrose. He is known to have sexually abused four boys between 1982 and 1992. He served at Holy Redeemer from 1982 through 1986. While there, he serially molested four brothers. He abused each boy until they reached puberty and then moved on to the next boy. Father Rick, as he was known, gained the family's trust and soon was taking the boys to basketball games and trips to San Diego and Washington, D.C. He attended pool parties and family barbecues even after he was transferred to another parish, and the molestation of these boys continued. Finally, after six years of abuse, one of the boys broke his silence. Testifying at the trial, Henry said, "I wish with all my heart that I could erase what I did with the boys—take it way, erase the past. I cannot." He was later accused of molesting up to thirteen during the years 1982 to 1992. One of the boys he molested committed suicide. Henry was eventually found guilty of molesting four boys in 1991. He served only three years of an eight-year sentence and was last reported living in Maryland. The one statement that is always heard with regards to Father Rick is: "He was always good with kids."

ARCHDIOCESE OF LOS ANGELES
CHILD ABUSE AND NEGLECT REPORTING FORM

☐ MANDATORY	☒ NON-MANDATORY
Date Reported to the Archdiocese:	8/17/2009 by REDACTED mother of victim
Reported to Archdiocese by:	8/25/2009 by victim
Alleged Victim :	REDACTED
Current Address:	
Telephone:	
Date of Birth:	REDACTED /1979
Alleged Perpetrator:	Msgr. Leland Boyer (RIP)
Reported Date of Incident: (s)	Various incidents from 1985 or 1986 to 1988 or 1989
Reported Circumstances of Incident(s):	REDACTED reports that he had many behavior problems as a child that started in early elementary school. He said that five years ago he told his therapist about abuse that he experienced at St. Bede's by Msgr. Boyer. Prior to that time he had seen many counselors but said he had blocked the memories. Then he had memories of three specific incidents that involved him standing in front of a mirror naked in the rectory and also vivid memories of the head board in the priest's room. The priest would either call REDACTED out of the classroom or ask him to his room after school when he was hanging out on the playground equipment after school. The abuse included fondling and penetration. REDACTED reported that the priest told him not to tell anyone because if he did "neither God nor his parents would love him" REDACTED also reports that the priest told him that these experiences were "between me, him and God and that God told him to do this" REDACTED believes the abuse stopped when he was in the fourth or fifth grade but does not know why it stopped then other than that he tried to avoid the priest as much as possible.
Reported Type of Abuse or Neglect:	Sexual Abuse
Reports to Public Authorities with dates:	Advised REDACTED of his right to report to authorities.
Comments:	REDACTED said there is another young man that had similar experiences with Msgr. Boyer and that he would encourage him to call Victims Assistance. I gave him an additional business card for the other young man.

This Archdiocese of Los Angeles document, released by court order in 2013, shows one of the allegations against Monsignor Boyer. *www.clergyfiles.la-archdiocese.org.*

Monsignor Leland Boyer

Monsignor Boyer became pastor of St. Bedes the Venerable Church in La Cañada in 1975 and stayed until his retirement in 1994. He was accused of molesting a thirteen-year-old La Cañada boy who came to him for help on a school project. After the encounter, Boyer wrote the boy a letter requesting his silence. In the letter, Boyer begged the boy not to tell anyone, saying that it would ruin him and that no one would believe the boy anyway. The boy later said, "I felt ashamed and was very scared." Church officials offered the boy therapy and asked that Boyer's contact with boys be restricted. At least one other boy claimed that Boyer molested him. After retiring, Boyer continued to profess his innocence. He was sued, but he died in 2005 before he had to face criminal charges.

Father Lynn Caffoe

Father Caffoe came to St. Bedes in 1982 and stayed until 1986. He was already under a cloud of suspicion when he arrived at St. Bedes. While at St. Callistus in Garden Grove, California, he was accused of molesting a boy. His superiors had issued a warning that his contact with young boys needed to be restricted. Father Caffoe was considered overly affectionate with the altar boys. While at St. Bedes, he allegedly videotaped naked boys in various states of sexual arousal. Despite warnings, his access to young boys was not restricted until 1991. The Los Angeles Archdiocese knew Caffoe had been accused of molesting minors between 1975 and 1991. His superiors ignored his possible criminal activities for sixteen years. In 2004, Cardinal Joeseph Ratzinger (later to become Pope Benedict) wrote Cardinal Mahoney and stated that Caffoe was a "master at manipulating people's feelings." Caffoe was not stripped of his priesthood. He died in 2009.

Father Christopher Kearny

Father Kearny taught at St. Francis High School in La Cañada from 1970 to 1995. He was accused of molesting a student during a wrestling match.

He was transferred to San Lorenzo Seminary in Santa Ynez, where he was again accused of molestation. Kearny allegedly staged wrestling matches in which the winner was the one who grabbed the other's testicles first. The school paid an out-of-court settlement, and Father Kearny was transferred for "health reasons."

Paul Kreutzer

On March 6, 2002, Paul Kreutzer was convicted of molesting ten girls over a thirty-year period. Kreutzer was a teacher and former president of the Santa Clarita Historical Society. As best can be determined, he began his career in 1968 at Holy Redeemer Church in Montrose, where he taught folk dancing. One woman testified in a Van Nuys court that at age ten, she had reported him to the principal of Our Lady of Peace in North Hills for molestation. Kreutzer also taught at Leggett Elementary School in Panorama City and Sunland Elementary. The prosecutor said, "He is a predator, and if he is ever set free…God help little girls and their families." Kreutzer had his defenders; two women testified on his behalf. One of the women stated, "I cannot tie the Paul that I know with the things that have been said about him. I love you Paul." Kreutzer was also accused of sexually exploiting two Vietnamese sisters that lived with him. His defense attorney, Rose Reglos, said, "Paul had very close relations with some of these girls. He treated them like his children, even helping to pay their college tuition. He still loves them." Supposedly, Kreutzer pled guilty to avoid putting the girls through the humiliation of a trial. He said in court, "I express sorrow for any such pain I have caused." He was sentenced to sixteen years plus nine consecutive one-year-to-life sentences. Mary-Ann Siefried said, "Thank God he is going to be off the street." He will be eligible for parole in 2025, at which time he will be eighty-six years old.

Rogelio Romero Gallardo

We should have known something was wrong with a man who drove a truck from Lake Elsinore to La Crescenta every day to go to work as a teacher at Crescenta Valley High School. Gallardo was a well-respected and well-liked ceramics teacher who had taught at Crescenta Valley High School for seven years. In 2005, he was charged with thirty-five counts of intent to distribute pornography, possession of child pornography and attempted destruction of evidence. The community was shocked to discover his secret life. The story broke when students found secret cameras in a faculty restroom that Gallardo allowed female students to use to change their clothes for ceramics class. Cameras were also found under the workbenches in the pottery room. It was discovered that Gallardo was uploading these videos to the Internet. The initial reaction at the school was one of disbelief and denial. Various reactions were:

"If I were hunting for someone to trust, Gallardo would be that guy."
"This surprises me."
"The fact that he has been accused is not enough evidence for me."
"That Rogelio is an awesome guy."

Once it sank in that the charges were true, anger was expressed over Gallardo's betrayal of student and faculty trust. He pled guilty to fifteen felony counts of distributing obscene material. He also pled guilty to seventeen misdemeanor charges of looking through a hole in the bathroom wall and the destruction of evidence. Gallardo faced up to twelve years in prison but was sentenced to three years. With credit for time served, he was expected to serve only ten and a half months. He is now required to register as a sex offender. Principal Linda Evans said, "We are glad that this chapter has been completed."

Michael Huber

Michael Huber, an aide to the Crescenta Valley High School's aquatics team and a youth pastor at the La Crescenta First Baptist Church, was arrested in March 2006 for possession of child pornography and was accused of molestation. Huber was charged with eight felony counts of abusing a minor for sex acts, two misdemeanor counts of possession of child pornography and two counts of misdemeanor child molestation. Huber's alleged victims were five boys under eighteen years of age. The purported crimes took place in 1998 and between 2000 and 2005. For more than twenty years, Huber had been an example of high Christian morals and devotion to community children. He had spoken to church groups and the PTA, impressing them with his understanding and compassion. At his trial, he claimed that he did not physically molest or touch boys and that the pictures in his possession were only for sexual fantasies. Huber was sentenced to four years and eight months for possession of child pornography.

Boy Scouts of America

In 1974, an investigation was launched into the actions of a forty-three-year-old bus driver. He had been on a Cub Scout committee in La Crescenta for six years. A Glendale police captain said, "He should be restricted from contact with boys."

Chapter 2
Prejudice

Racial Hostility in the Foothills

The 1920s was a period of racial tension in the United States, and the Foothills and the surrounding areas were not exempt. The term "Sundowner Cities" applied to Glendale and ten thousand other towns in America. It meant that no blacks were allowed in town after dark. In one instance in the late 1960s, an African American nurse was told that her husband would not be able to pick her up from work in Glendale, as Glendale law forbade blacks in the city after dark. There never was such a law, but Glendale Police acted as if it there were. During this period, African Americans driving through the Crescenta Valley from Pacoima to Pasadena were frequently stopped by police to discourage their travel on Foothill Boulevard.

The first instance of the Ku Klux Klan (KKK) or "Invisible Empire" dates back to 1866 in Tennessee, founded under the leadership of Nathan Bedford Forrest, a former slave owner and Confederate general. This group officially disbanded in 1869 because Forrest claimed that it had been taken over by evil men for immoral purposes. But the Klan and its activities continued until the 1890s. The second Klan was founded in 1915 for "the protection of womanhood, the fatherhood of God and the brotherhood of man." The phrase "brotherhood of man" should have been written as "brotherhood of white men." This second Klan grew to a membership of 3 million individuals in the 1920s. The Klan was opposed to African-Americans, Jews, Catholics, unions, birth control and evolution. It was 110 percent for white gentile fundamentalist Protestants. A large Klan gathering in Glendale occurred on July 12, 1924, when the Glendale Klaven hosted the Los Angeles Klaven at Verdugo Park for a barbecue picnic and baseball game. Glendale won by pitching superior "kurve" balls. (In Klan vocabulary, a "k" was required to be used in place of a "c.") As dusk fell, the hooded Klansmen followed a man on horseback carrying a fiery cross. They marched into the San Rafael Hills above Glendale College to the site that now houses the Child Development Center, where three hundred worthy "aliens" were initiated into the Klan when the "Exalted Cyclops" gave the signal for the "Nighthawk" to bring the inductees forward. This ceremony was attended by three thousand Klansmen and an estimated fifteen thousand spectators. A good time was had by one and all.

In the 1930s, the Klan served as a bridge between nativist and fascist groups. On August 18, 1940, a formal alliance was formed with the German American Bund. This took place at the Nazi encampment Nordlund in Andover, New Jersey. This alliance lasted seventeen months before ending on December 7, 1941. It is important to remember that all racist groups are basically the same. The names change, but ideologies are interchangeable. Their common denominator is hatred.

In 1936, Klan membership was a problem at Glendale Community College, where it was rumored that freshmen had formed a secret group known as the "Klansmen." This was also the year that Pasadena City College (PCC) played Glendale Community College (GCC) for the league football championship. Jackie Robinson led PCC to victory. He was rewarded by a physical attack from GCC players. His injuries were sufficient to require hospitalization.

On December 16, 1939, five people were arrested for passing out KKK literature in Glendale.

In September 1966, William V. Fowler, the "Grand Cyclops" of the California KKK and former minister of the Covenant Church of Jesus Christ, fought successfully for the reorganization of the Klan. Fowler was a resident of La Crescenta living on Mayfield Avenue. Although the Klan had been declared an illegal organization in 1946, a judge allowed the group to reorganize. When asked about his decision, the judge replied, "People have a constitutional right to be stupid. If they want to put sheets on their heads and act like children, they have that right." Fowler planned a Foothills rally we say, "hands off," and we will defend this institution against every enemy, whether it be political or ecclesiastical.

V. CHRISTIAN IDEALS

1. We magnify the Bible—as the basis of our Constitution, the foundation of our government, the source of our laws, the sheet-anchor of our liberties, the most practical guide of right living, and the source of all true wisdom.

2. We teach the worship of God. For we have in mind the divine command, "Thou shalt worship the Lord thy God."

3. We honor the Christ, as the Klansman's only criterion of character. And we seek at His hands that cleansing from sin and impurity, which only He can give.

4. We believe that the highest expression of life is in service and in sacrifice for that which is right; that selfishness can have no place in a true Klansman's life and character; but that he must be moved by unselfish motives, such as characterized our Lord the Christ and moved Him to the highest service and the supreme sacrifice for that which was right.

I have but suggested here a few of the many ideals of the Ku Klux Klan. Let us seek to make these real in our life and practice so that we may become bright, true Klansmen, and be ready for other ideals and principles as they shall be presented from time to time.

For more information contact the State Chairman of the Calif. Knights of the Ku Klux Klan.
Rev. Wm. V. Fowler P.O Box 312
La Crescenta, Calif.

IDEALS

OF THE

KU KLUX KLAN

A

California Committee

WE have been passing through the formative period of the organization, and now we have come to the period of constructive planning and activity. We must know what we are, and the things for which we stand in order that our activity may rightly contribute to the upbuilding of character and of a high-grade citizenship. The time has now come when the world will know the Ku Klux Klan in its true character. Before we can correctly interpret this Order and the things for which it stands we ourselves must know ourselves, and the principles and ideals of this Order.

This 1966 brochure stating the "Ideals of the Ku Klux Klan" was produced in and issued from the Crescenta Valley. The state chairman of the California KKK (the "Cyclops" in the Klan hierarchy) lived on Mayfield Avenue in La Crescenta. *Glendale Public Library.*

for September 19, 1966. When the community expressed opposition, Fowler pledged that "bloodshed" would take place if any opposition appeared. Fowler estimated that five thousand people would attend his rally. He was disappointed when only one hundred supporters appeared. However, three hundred people showed up in opposition.

In April 1968, an interracial couple received a warning not to move into a neighborhood in Tujunga. There was an attempted cross burning, and as a result, the couple did not move.

In the late 1970s, John Mayfield, an African American male, enrolled at Crescenta Valley High School. His family had moved here so he could play for Crescenta Valley High's championship basketball team. The family's home was vandalized. John Clark, a woodshop teacher at Crescenta Valley High, took a student crew to repair the damage. While there, Clark discovered the neighbor who had caused the damage, as he sported a Confederate flag in his window. Before he left the area, Clark informed the bigot that there were two thousand students at Crescenta Valley High who liked John Mayfield and they might take it badly if Mayfield's home was vandalized again. The racist neighbor moved shortly thereafter.

The Klan never dies. In the 1980s, the KKK in Sunland-Tujunga offered to provide arms to "good white citizens" for the purpose of handling the gang problem. The Klan's solution to the gang problem was to shoot the gang members on sight. In 1983, ten robed Klansmen passed out leaflets for an hour in Sunland. On December 3, 1983, white supremacists belonging to several different organizations burned three eighteen-foot-tall crosses in Kegal Canyon, a racially mixed neighborhood just north of Lake View Terrace. Richard Butler and Tom Metzger also participated. Butler was the commander of the Idaho-based group Aryan Nations. Metzger, the former "Grand Dragon" of the KKK, was also a former member of White Aryan Resistance (WAR). Metzger was the most renowned of these men. He had run for Congress on the Democratic ticket in 1980. He had also been convicted for inciting skinheads to murder an Ethiopian immigrant in Portland, Oregon. In this case, a $12.5 million civil judgment was pronounced against Metzger. He found it amusing that the judgment impoverished him and forced him onto the welfare rolls. Other illustrious participants included David Tale, a convicted murderer of a Missouri State Trooper, and Randall Evans and Frank Silva, who were convicted of conspiracy in the murder of Alan Berg, a Denver talk-show host.

The trial of Metzger, Stanley Wittick, Brad Kelly and Eric Schmidt took place in June 1981. They were tried for conspiracy to violate the fire code, which was a felony. They were also tried on two misdemeanors: unlawful burning and unlawful assembly. Metzger was sentenced to six months in jail, three years probation and three hundred hours of community service. He served two months and was released to care for his ill wife.

In 1988, the Pullman Café on North Brand in Glendale, owned by A.O. Flowers, an African American woman, was vandalized. Painted on the building were the words "The nigger is both an economic and social menace to society." In 1992, Glendale High School suspended eleven seniors for vandalism and passing out racist fliers on campus that read, "We need more white people in Glendale and the KKK."

RACIAL COVENANTS

On April 14, 1941, the Foothills were called to arms as the *Ledger* announced, "Race Restriction—Mass Meeting." The president of the La Cañada Chamber of Commerce, Frank Lanterman, urged a large turnout. He wrote, "We are confronted with a serious situation in the La Cañada valley. A colored family is negotiating for the purchase of a home in this locality." The *Ledger* editorial stated that the people of La Cañada, Montrose, La Crescenta and Sunland-Tujunga would meet to discuss racial restrictions. The editorial's phrasing is wonderful: "We are privileged to choose our neighbors for our mutual protection. [When] folks of one race force their way amongst other racial groups," the native racial groups "have the right to avoid possible unpleasantries by prevention, rather than cure the problem by other methods." The editorial does not define what it means by "unpleasantries" or "other methods." Designed for exclusionary segregationist purposes, racial covenants restricted the sale of property to most non-white members of a community. While they primarily targeted African Americans, they were also aimed against Mexican Americans, Asian Americans and Jewish Americans. In Fresno, Armenians faced racial covenants.

The 1917 court ruling *Buchanan v. Warley* declared racial covenants unconstitutional. While this ruling made statutes illegal, it failed to outlaw private agreements between realtors and property owners. From the 1920s through the 1940s, private agreements or racially restricted covenants exploded throughout Los Angeles. In *Bound for Freedom*, author Douglas Flamming outlines the typical racial covenant: "At no time should said premises or any part thereof or any building erected thereon be sold, occupied, let, leased or given to anyone of any race other than the Caucasian." Flamming also explains the systematic process of making these covenants a norm in real estate practices. The Federal Housing Administration, which made home ownership possible for countless white families, actively discriminated against minorities attempting to purchase homes in white communities. As

Abe's Lock and Key, which has been a fixture in the valley for over ninety years, is unusual not in its longevity but in the fact that it has always been a black-owned business in an almost entirely white community. When the original Abe started a shoeshine and locksmith shop on Honolulu Avenue in the early 1920s, he could own a business here but not a home. *Glendale Public Library.*

Said deed further provides for reversion of title upon breach of the following provisions:- "That the parties of second part shall not convey, sell or lease or otherwise dispose of said premises, or any part thereof to any person not of the White or Caucasian race, nor shall any person other than of the White or Caucasian race acquire said property or any portion thereof or any interest therein by purchase, lease or otherwise."

This is an actual example of a racial covenant written into the deed of a home in La Crescenta in the 1920s. This was not an unusual clause during that time period. *Historical Society of the Crescenta Valley.*

the population of Los Angeles was increasingly segregated, the communities to the north reserved a place for minorities only as domestic servants. These workers oftentimes were required to leave their work areas before sunset. "Sundown cities," as they were known, implemented written and unwritten codes that forbade any person of color from being within the city limits after dark. Glendale shared similar attitudes. During that period in our history, William McMillan, then president of the Glendale Realty Board, said, "The Glendale Realty Board and the Glendale Brokers as a whole cooperate in every way to keep Glendale an All-American city. By enforcing race restrictions, we have been able to keep our standard well up to the front ranks of All-American." Given such views, it is not surprising that Glendale's population of 62,736 in 1930 was overwhelmingly Caucasian, with the African American population listed as 38. In 1940, Glendale's population was 82,000, with only 68 African Americans. In the 1960s census, the African American population had dropped to 60. In the post–World War II era, racial restrictions began to slowly disappear, but Glendale remained a bastion of traditional values, and many residents practiced outright racism. According to Glendale historian Juliette M. Arroyo, "The real racism began when Glendale prided itself as the fastest growing city in America" as increasing residential subdivisions continued to prohibit real estate sales to African Americans. A person who left Glendale in 1967 and returned to the city today would not believe its current racial diversity.

Black Work Crews Rejected by Crescenta Valley

In the pre–World War II years, racially exclusive Crescenta Valley soundly rejected the establishment of a local all-black Civilian Conservation Corps (CCC) camp not once but twice—in 1935 and again in 1941.

The CCC was part of President Roosevelt's New Deal, designed to lift America out of the Great Depression. It was probably the most popular of Roosevelt's programs, as it demanded work from those receiving welfare. Operating from 1933 to 1942, the program enlisted out-of-work men aged seventeen to twenty-three in labor projects related to conservation and natural resources. The young men received military-style discipline and training, which resulted in improved physical conditioning and heightened morale. They also received wages: thirty dollars per month, twenty-five of which was sent directly to their families at home. Two and a half million boys became men during the course of the program, which arguably helped ready America for World War II.

The CCC boys did great work, providing the muscle for building mountain roads, draining swamps and planting trees. Locally, they were the backbone of the firefighting efforts in the Pickens Canyon Fire of 1933, and in the New Year's Flood of 1934, they were local heroes in rescue and cleanup efforts. We had three such camps locally: Tuna Camp, now the Verdugo Hills Golf Course; San Antonio Camp in Deer Canyon in the Verdugos; and another in Hall Beckley Canyon in La Cañada. Each camp housed about two hundred CCC boys.

Although they were initially racially integrated, public and internal pressure to segregate resulted in the creation of separate white and black CCC companies. The all-black companies received hostile receptions from many of the communities near their camps.

And so it was in 1935 that the all-white company at Tuna Camp was rotated out and an all-black company was ordered to take its place. Opposition to the plan was led by the local chamber of commerce, but once the news hit the local paper, hundreds of letters went out to the CCC's leadership. Every organization and club in the valley, including the PTA, the Republican and Democratic clubs and the ominously named La Crescenta Protective Association, sent letters of protest to the local commander of the CCC. We can assume that the community's objections were not based on the work the black CCC recruits would be doing—mostly backcountry wilderness work. It was more likely the idea that in their off-hours, the two hundred-some young black men would descend on Montrose for some R&R.

The CCC had a policy of not forcing communities to accept the all-black companies, and so the transfer of the "negro" company was held up until the community could be consulted. The chief ranger of the U.S. Forest Service made a personal phone call from Washington to the head of the Crescenta Chamber asking him to withdraw the organization's opposition, but to no avail. The CCC backed down, and an all-white CCC company was brought into Tuna Camp instead.

In early 1941, the scenario was played out again at Tuna Camp. A black company was slated to occupy the camp, but the same opposition was put up by the community. This time, they framed their argument in terms of the community's efforts to restrict the use and occupancy of property locally to only those of the Caucasian race. The drive to place the black company in

Tuna Camp was dropped, and the young men were instead transferred to San Diego.

At this point, the CCC as a whole was winding down, as defense jobs were readily available to the young men who had relied on the CCC for employment. Tuna Camp was temporarily closed. Just a few months later, on December 8, 1941, Tuna Camp was reopened by the government, and a tall barbed-wire fence was strung around the barracks of the camp. The following week, hundreds of Japanese nationals and Japanese Americans were herded into the camp at gunpoint for interrogation before being shipped to internment camps or federal prisons. So much for local opposition to "occupancy by races other than Caucasian" at Tuna Camp.

JEWISH LIFE IN OLD CRESCENTA VALLEY

The early settlers of Crescenta Valley were mostly wealthy Midwesterners, along with immigrants from Germany, Italy and other European countries—all of whom were white and predominantly Protestant or Catholic. Those of differing color, ethnic background or faith had problems being accepted, and early valley residents of the Jewish faith faced that problem in La Crescenta.

Jerry Weinberg, an early member of the Jewish community in the valley, related that his family moved to the valley in the late 1920s and felt culturally isolated. One day, they participated in a tree-planting project in Montrose. When little Jerry spoke some words of Yiddish to his mother, one of the tree-planting supervisors overheard and enthusiastically jumped into the conversation. The Jewish "Goldie" Goldstein was working locally as a forest ranger, and he and the Weinbergs became fast friends. Jerry told me that as a kid, he was shunned by many neighborhood kids, and some parents prevented their children from playing with him because of his Jewish roots. He also related that the small enclave of local Jews was uncomfortably aware of the German American Bund, the American arm of the Nazi Party, whose members were sometimes part of the weekend celebrations at Hindenburg Park in the 1930s.

By 1955, the Jewish community in the valley had grown large enough to warrant the construction of the Crescenta Valley Jewish Center at 3966 Pennsylvania. About one hundred families became members, but for unknown reasons, the center closed sometime in the '60s. Today, the building is a Montessori school with a conspicuously bright paint job.

In 1955, the Crescenta Valley Jewish Center was built at the intersection of Honolulu and Pennsylvania Avenues to serve about one hundred local Jewish families. The building is still there and now houses a Montessori school. *Photo by Mike Lawler.*

A more recent view of Jewish life in Crescenta Valley comes from La Crescenta native John Drayman. He related that his father, Jay Drayman, a clothing manufacturer, moved to Los Angeles in 1949 seeking a drier climate for his wife, Dale. He was attracted to Glendale because of its great schools, but as he was house hunting, several homes he made offers on were mysteriously taken off the market or inexplicably fell out of escrow. He was finally able to purchase a home in the valley outside the Glendale borders that was relatively free of the racial and ethnic covenants so typical of many Glendale properties at the time. As a businessman, Jay was active in the community, and like other businessmen, he was anxious to network. He was encouraged to apply for a membership to the Oakmont Country Club by a close friend and local developer who had built the Glenwood Oaks tract. However, Jay was denied membership and told by the membership committee that his religion was the reason. Interestingly, the son of the man who blackballed John's father later became one of John's closest friends and recounted to him the details of this act of prejudice.

For Jewish families in the '60s, there was still a sense of threat—unspoken but tangible despite the enactment of the Civil Rights Act. By the time John was a teenager in the '70s, local anti-Semitism was far less overt and seemed to surface only when folks of a "certain generation" got angry. He remembered that as a kid selling Christmas cards door to door, he once had a disagreement over a misspelling approved and initialed by a customer. She ended the argument by calling him a "dirty Jew." Drayman also suffered a beating at the Keyhole public pool during the Six-Day War by older boys whose parents told John he should "go to Israel to fight alongside the other Jews."

Drayman believes that things have changed for the better and that Crescenta Valley is today a tolerant and inclusive place. We like to think that the bias that American Jews faced in our community is now history. But history often repeats. Today, the Armenian American community, which shares a similar background of genocide, diaspora and immigration with the Jewish people, struggles for acceptance in the Crescenta Valley, just as the Jews did before them.

GERALD L.K. SMITH

Glendale was home to another well-known racist who associated with the Bund and other right-wing groups. Gerald L.K. Smith published *The Cross and the Flag* on South Brand in Glendale. The magazine, which was associated with sixty other right-wing racist publications, was the official publication of the Christian Nationalist Crusade. Smith was active for over forty years and is considered to be the godfather of almost all prominent racists alive today. He always rejected the charge that he was prejudiced, claiming that prejudice was un-Christian and he was, in fact, a Christian. He claimed that it was a proven fact that African Americans were inferior to whites. Smith was an imposing figure and, according to Huey Long, "…was, after me, the best rabble-rouser in the country." H.L. Menken said that Smith was the "gutsiest and goriest, the deadliest and damndest orator ever heard on this or any other earth."

Smith began his ministries in Soldier's Cove, Wisconsin, in a Disciples of Christ Church in 1923. In 1929, he moved to Shreveport, Louisiana, where he worked with the KKK and was briefly a member of William Dudley Pelly's "Silver Shirts." In 1934, he went to work for Huey P. Long and the Share the Wealth movement. He was standing next to Long when Long was assassinated. After Long's murder, Smith took over Share the Wealth and allied himself with Father Charles Choughlin and Francis Townsend. In

The Cross and the Flag was started by Reverend Gerald L. K. Smith in 1942 as an eight-page monthly magazine. It ran until 1977 and at one time had twenty-five thousand subscribers. The magazine featured articles with such titles as "The Jews and Their Lies" and "Integration Is Genocide." *www.encyclopediaofarkansas.net.*

1942, he started *The Cross and the Flag* to replace Father Choughlin's defunct journal, *Social Justice*. Smith founded the America First Party in 1944 and was its first presidential candidate. He received 1,030 votes in that election. In 1948, after his endorsement by Strom Thurman was rejected, he ran again and received only 48 votes.

In 1950, Smith came to Glendale. He endorsed Earl Warren for governor, an endorsement that was rejected by Warren. He attacked Eisenhower as being Jewish and backed Los Angeles mayoral candidate Norris Poulson, who also rejected the endorsement. In 1963, he endorsed Thomas Kuchel for U.S. senator and again had his endorsement rebuffed. In the 1964 presidential election, he endorsed Barry Goldwater. It is unknown if Goldwater even took notice. In 1964, Smith moved to Eureka Springs, Arkansas, to build a religious theme park called "Christ of the Ozarks." He was unable to build the theme park, but he did build the second-largest statue of Christ in the Americas. Smith returned to Glendale in the 1970s.

In the early '70s, a Glendale student was doing a term paper on Gerald L.K. Smith and made an appointment to interview the famous racist. Smith agreed to the meeting but declined to be interviewed when he discovered the male student had shoulder-length hair. Smith died in Glendale in April 1976. As best can be determined, the last action of the Christian National Crusade was the picketing by two of its elderly members of the Academy Awards ceremony the year it gave a lifetime achievement award to Charlie Chaplin. The group officially disbanded on December 23, 1977.

J.D. STONER

In November 1987, J.D. Stoner came to speak in Glendale. Stoner was a KKK member and a convicted murderer, having bombed an African American church in Birmingham, Alabama. This was considered one of the most horrific acts of the civil rights era, as four little girls died in the bombing. It took the justice system twenty-five years to find Stoner guilty. He was given a ten-year sentence for the murders, but he served only five years and three months. Stoner met with only 12 supporters at the Glendale Holiday Inn that November day. There were 250 protestors present. Two fifteen-year-old neo-Nazis were attacked by the crowd.

Chapter 3
Drugs and Alcohol

The Wicked Past of Whiting Woods

The little neighborhood of Whiting Woods is one of the most sedate and beautiful areas in the entire valley. Its shaded streets wind up and around a beautiful canyon tucked into the folds of the green Verdugo Mountains. Native oaks and sycamore trees shade the large rambling homes built there. Two architectural gems are located in Whiting Woods: a Richard Neutra house and another designed by architect John Lautner. Whiting Woods is a great place to live—but that wasn't always the case. It has a history that covers nearly every vice of twentieth-century living.

Whiting Woods is named for Perry Whiting, a self-made millionaire, who bought the little canyon as a place to enjoy nature and solitude. He left us an autobiography that gives us some of the ugly details of the origins of Whiting Woods.

When Whiting first encountered the property in 1915, it was the home of the Pasadena Mountain Club, a lofty title, but in reality just a bar and whorehouse. There was a small "clubhouse" where the booze was served, as well as ten tiny shacks in back for the other "club activities." For fifty cents, a customer could buy a club membership, which allowed him to drink at the bar in the clubhouse and use the club's facilities. We can assume the other on-site "business transactions" were performed by female "independent contractors." The club was closed by the district attorney under the Red Light Abatement Act, and as Whiting held a lien on the property, he was able to acquire the "club grounds" (the east side of the canyon). As an interesting side note, a current resident of Whiting Woods whose home sits near the site of the old clubhouse reported the discovery of scores of old whiskey bottles buried in his yard.

Whiting probably thought the oak-covered land around the old clubhouse would make a good getaway spot. So it was with consternation that he noted an ad in the newspaper stating that an investor had plans to subdivide 415 acres on the opposite side of the canyon with the intention of establishing chicken ranches on the gorgeous wooded slopes. Ever the savvy businessman, Whiting was able to block the development plans and pick up that acreage for $14,000. He now owned both slopes of the canyon.

In 1918, Whiting, having business elsewhere, rented the old clubhouse/bar to a man who planned to run it as a restaurant. In reality, however, it was run as a roadhouse speakeasy, as were other "restaurants" tucked away in our canyons during Prohibition, kept well supplied by the many moonshiners who operated in Crescenta Valley. It was at this speakeasy that one of the more spectacular murders in our local history took place, in which a black man, working for both the moonshiners and the police as an informant, shot down a white man during an exchange of racial slurs and threats of revenge for the informant's double-dealing.

The last piece of the canyon that Whiting needed in order to own it outright was the canyon floor itself. This 260-acre lush meadow was owned by an old Chinese man known simply as John. John had some vegetable gardens, well watered from the creek that ran through the meadow, as did other Chinese truck farmers up and down the Verdugo Canyon. But his business was also opium sales, presumably to the other Chinese farmers and laborers in the valley and the odd American hooked on "chasing the dragon." In 1922, Whiting was able to convince John that he could retire back to China in luxury if he were to sell his land. John wisely did, and Whiting now owned the whole canyon.

In 1926, Whiting, now with his own little piece of paradise, built the classic "big white house on the hill" on the western side of the canyon. In the '50s, the Whiting Woods development took shape around the old mansion's site, on its way to becoming the desirable and relatively law-abiding neighborhood it is today. It's intriguing to reflect on this wicked past as you drive up the shady, quiet streets of Whiting Woods.

RELICS OF BOOTLEGGING IN CRESCENTA VALLEY

During Prohibition, Crescenta Valley was close enough to Los Angeles to help supply the demand for bootleg liquor but far enough away to be out of sight to the law. Our deep, shadowy canyons provided many out-of-the-way spots where moonshiners could produce their goods. Since the valley below had been cultivated largely in grape vineyards, the moonshiners had plenty to work with. The area was a hotbed of illegal alcohol production. Some of the local ranch houses had wine production areas that were fairly hidden, as well as secret storage areas where the booze could be stashed.

Those areas are occasionally discovered in older homes today. Crescenta Valley resident Randy Sims remembered going to a friend's house back in the '60s—one of those stone houses on the north end of Montrose. His buddy mentioned that he had something cool to show Randy in the basement. As they stepped down into the basement, the friend jumped up, grabbed the beam above him, planted his feet firmly against the concrete back wall and pushed hard. A section of the concrete wall swung slowly

The deep-wooded canyons of the Verdugo Mountains were perfect spots for both the production and sale of moonshine during Prohibition. They were conveniently close to Los Angeles and Glendale yet remote enough to be out of the eyes of the law. This shot shows La Crescenta Elementary School in the foreground and what is today Whiting Woods in the background. *Glendale Public Library.*

In this shot for the local newspapers from the 1920s, Montrose sheriffs and law officials dump confiscated moonshine into the gutter in front of the Montrose Sheriff's Station on Ocean View Boulevard, just north of Honolulu Avenue. *Glendale Public Library*.

According to local lore, the Trail Café at 2206 Honolulu had the dubious distinction of being the first place locally to serve alcohol when Prohibition ended in 1934—"dubious" because many claim that it was serving alcohol before Prohibition ended as well. *Glendale Public Library.*

inward, revealing a concrete room about five feet wide and running the length of the house.

Randy's friend said his parents had only found it when they accidently discovered a large steel lever hidden under a rug in the dining room. When they pulled it, it unlocked this secret room directly below. It was empty now, but when they first discovered it, it had the decaying remains of a still, several empty jars and a cot. One end of the long room ended in a short dirt tunnel that came to the surface behind the house in some thick bushes.

A more recent discovery was made by Stuart Byles, a local contractor and vice-president of the Historical Society of Crescenta Valley. Stuart was doing some work on one of the old houses near La Crescenta Avenue and Foothill when he got talking to a neighbor who was living in a 1920s-style home. When Stuart told him about his interest in local history, the neighbor said, "I've got to show you this!"

An exterior stairway from the neighbor's second story came down next to his garage. Below the landing of the stairway was a secret door, which Stuart had to get down on hands and knees to see. A hidden latch opened the small door, and Stuart and the neighbor crawled down into an eight-foot-high basement under the garage. Scattered around were a dozen ancient wine carboys, some sealed, with remnants of what must have once been wine. The back wall had a bricked-up hole in it, and the neighbor explained it had been a tunnel just big enough to crawl through. The tunnel went across his yard and into the yard next door before eventually emerging in the floor of the neighbor's garage, which had since been torn down.

Stuart and the neighbor then entered the main house and went down the steps into a full-sized basement. In that basement was a closet, and hidden in the floorboards of the closet was a trapdoor. Opening that revealed another set of steep stairs descending into yet another basement, about half the size of the one above. This was a heck of a big working space for a house of this size. It was obvious this house had been the center of an ambitious booze-making operation during the Prohibition years.

Drugs

The role of drugs in the Foothills is too extensive to be covered fully in a work of this length. We can say that the San Gabriel Mountains have proven to be very productive in the cultivation of marijuana, as extensive plantations are frequently discovered by police. Following are some of the more noteworthy stories about drugs in the Crescenta Valley.

The first mention of drugs in the Foothills goes back to the 1920s, when opium was reportedly grown and sold by a Chinese man in the canyon that is today Whiting Woods.

In November 1993, sheriff's deputies arrested thirty students from La Cañada High School and seventeen students at a local continuation high school. Police officers went undercover at the schools to identify students as users and sellers. This was the second raid at La Cañada High School. All students arrested were released to their parents later that same day and suffered a five-day suspension.

On October 17, 2007, five thousand marijuana plants were seized in the Verdugo Mountains by the Glendale Police Department, which was working with twelve other police agencies. The marijuana plantation was a sophisticated operation. It utilized water stored in remote cisterns for fire control, and the growers were using an environmentally friendly drip irrigation system. The drought conditions in 2007 proved to be the undoing of the operation. It turned out that the lush greenery of the plantation stood out against the barren conditions of the surrounding mountains. Police said that the farm spread out over two or three acres and was two years old. It was located above Crescenta Valley Park. The estimated value of the crop was $10 million. Illegal marijuana cultivation is a danger in the foothill area. Due to the value of the crop, people tend to guard and protect their product at all costs. During this raid, police discovered sleeping bags and rifles with sniper scopes and live ammunition.

On March 12, 2009, local police arrested four people and seized thirty-two and a half pounds of opium. The opium had been sent to an apartment in Glendale. Its point of origin was Armenia. Lieutenant Bruce Fox of the Special Investigative Bureau of the Glendale Police Department placed the street value of the opium at $500,000. Fox, a Crescenta Valley High School graduate, said that the contents of the apartment indicated that the suspects had been involved in drug trafficking for some time. Two months prior to this discovery, police had seized twenty-eight pounds of opium hidden in a woman's pants.

On March 25, 2010, Glendale Police chief Ron DePompa discussed Crescenta Valley's drug and gang problem at a Crescenta Valley High School faculty meeting. DePompa referred to a gang known as 211C and showed mug shots of gang members from La Crescenta and Montrose. These men had been arrested on suspicion of strong-arm robbery and witness intimidation. 211C started as a tagging crew and grew into a gang. DePompa said that the founding members lived on Mary Street just north of the Crescenta Valley High School campus. The author, Gary Keyes, remembered the location well from the times he had driven the Crescenta Valley High School security car after school: "The house was always a problem, with large numbers of kids hanging out after school. One time, we were especially concerned with the house and cruised by it multiple times. We were flagged down by undercover officers, who informed us that they were trying to make arrests but that our security car was spooking the dealers and making it hard for the officers to observe their activities. We were asked to drive somewhere else." This was at a time before there was much gang activity in the Foothills. Police speaking at the faculty meeting stated that before 2007, they could pull up to an intersection in our valley and tell the students, "Those smoking dope go to the right, those not, to the left," and the kids were naïve enough to comply.

During the 2008–10 school years, twenty-four Crescenta Valley High School students were expelled and fifty-seven suspended for drug and alcohol use. In December 2010, four hundred marijuana plants were confiscated on a raid on two businesses in the 2500 block of Honolulu Boulevard in Montrose. The location was a clothing store and the Blue Seas Travel Agency. The street value of the plants was placed at $200,000. On September 18, 2011, *Glendale News Press* reported that there had been forty-one expulsions for drug-related offenses between 2006 and 2011. This was twice the rate for Glendale High School and three times the rate for Hoover High School. Three CVHS students were arrested in 2010–11. Two were picked up for drugs and one for weapons. Veronica Rocha of the *Glendale News Press* stated that the drug arrests in January were heroin related. Chief DePompa stated that a Hollywood-based gang played a major role in supplying the drugs in our area. He also noted that one of the problems for area police was the number of eighteen- to twenty-five-year-olds who had prescriptions for medicinal marijuana. At this time, there were marijuana dispensaries in Sunland and Tujunga.

The drug problem in the Foothills eventually led to the formation of the Crescenta Valley Drug and Alcohol Prevention Coalition. The coalition defined the drug problem and currently works on education and prevention. It cooperates with governmental agencies, educators, local businesses and residents to fight the use of drugs in our community. In addition, Crescenta Valley High School issued an extensive self-study report in March 2012. On May 24, 2012, the *Glendale News Press* reported that on that date, three men with ties to a Montrose hydroponics business were arrested after police seized nine hundred marijuana plants. Narcotics sergeant Luis Pasache said that the warehouse operation was a very sophisticated affair. Glendale Police Department's Lieutenant Scott Bickle said, "The business, Green Light Hydroponics in the 2600 block of Honolulu Avenue, had been under investigation for months." The hydroponics business's slogan was "Our Business Is Growing." In addition to the plants seized, police recovered thirty pounds of marijuana, $50,000 in cash, two firearms and parts of a grenade launcher.

On July 25, 2013, Mary O'Keefe of the *Crescenta Valley Weekly* reported that Glendale police found forty pounds of methamphetamines during a routine traffic stop at the Lowell and La Tuna Canyon exit off the 210 Freeway. During the traffic stop, it was determined that the driver, Carlos Gutierrez of San Jose, had an outstanding arrest warrant for failure to appear. The K-9 unit was brought in and indicated several spots on the car for further investigation. Police found several clear plastic bags hidden behind the inner side panels. The arrested men, of course, claimed no knowledge of the presence of the drugs. They were held on $500,000 bail each.

On September 6, 2013, Mary O'Keefe reported that Crescenta Valley Sheriff's Deputies arrested ten people at a home on Gertrude Avenue in La Crescenta. Neighbors had noticed unusual activities at the house and had alerted the police. Police identified the house as a dispersal site—a place where marijuana was packaged and then shipped out. Marijuana, $30,000 in cash and one firearm were found in the house.

In concluding the story of drugs in the Foothills, the *Glendale News Press* reported that the police arrested Gevork Hakopian at his La Crescenta home in the 2700 block in Los Olivos on September 27, 2012. Ten pounds of opium were recovered at the location. Hakopian was arrested on charges of possessing and packaging for distribution. The street value of the opium was estimated at $42,000.

Chapter 4
War

The Foothills During World War II

During World War II, Foothill Boulevard doubled as a military highway. General Patton's tanks probably passed through the community on the way to the Mojave Desert to train. Foothill was often closed to civilian traffic. In fact, there was little civilian traffic allowed anywhere during the war. Wartime gasoline rationing limited a driver with an "A" sticker to only three gallons of gas a week. Antiaircraft guns were also placed throughout the valley. One antiaircraft battery was located on Reynolds Hill, just above the Foothill Car Wash in La Crescenta. Another was located in a debris basin on Cross Street, also in La Crescenta. Yet another was located in the Verdugo Hills near Oakmont Country Club. La Cañada Intermediate School served as a refueling station for trucks and jeeps heading toward the harbor to be shipped to the war zones or desert training centers. At the present-day site of Mount Gleason Intermediate School was a large military installation.

In 1945, two thousand German POWs were quartered at the Los Angeles County Fairgrounds to pick oranges. Lockheed, in Burbank, was making a major contribution to the war effort in airplane production, and test flights were routinely conducted over the Crescenta Valley. The gun sights of the planes were sighted by firing a few rounds at targets on the Verdugo

A typical wartime family living in Montrose during World War II: Velma, Floyd and Tex Farrar. Velma worked swing shift at Lockheed building P-38s, while Tex joined the Seabees to build frontline airstrips in the Pacific Theater. *Floyd Farrar.*

Mountains. In all, Lockheed produced 9,423 P-38s, 500 F-4s, 2,857 B-17s, 535 P2Vs and 14 C-69s during the war. In Glendale, the Grand Central Flying School trained U.S. Army Air Corps pilots and Royal Air Force pilots. A squadron of P-38s was based there for coastal defense.

The German-American Bund

Members of the German-American Bund considered themselves loyal, patriotic Americans. Their heroes were Washington, Lincoln and Horst-Wessel, a Nazi storm trooper who was killed in a 1930s street brawl in Germany. Bund rallies featured pictures of George Washington next to swastikas. The Bund was a proponent for the U.S. Constitution, the American flag and white gentiles. It was opposed to Jewish/Communist plots, blacks and immoral influences like jazz. One of its greatest targets was "Jewish-controlled Hollywood" and the movies it produced. The Bund promoted boycotts of Jewish-run businesses and slandered teachers who opposed it. The group wanted to produce a "pure" United States that was free of Jews, minorities and Communists.

During the depression of the 1930s, some Americans turned to extremist organizations to improve their economic positions. Considering the depths of the depression, it is surprising how small these extremist groups actually were. These groups included Communists, Technocrats, Townsendites, the Share the Wealth movement and the Bund. The western headquarters of the Bund was Deutsch Haus, located in the 600 block of West Fifteenth Street in Los Angeles. The Los Angeles Bund had an Aryan bookstore and radio station, KRKD. The station broadcast a show called the *German Hour*, in which the hosts attacked Jews and Communists, whom they considered the twin enemies of Germany and "Amerika."

In La Crescenta, the Bund held its rallies in Hindenburg Park, which was located on the western edge of what is now La Crescenta Park. The park was used by the local German community to celebrate German culture and fellowship. It contained statues of German cultural heroes such as President Paul Von Hindenburg, as well as a chalet where sausage and beer was served. It was one of several recreational areas used by the Bund. Local historian Charles Basuback died too soon for the Historical Society of Crescenta Valley to record all of his recollections of the history of our valley. That grand old man had a photographic memory. In discussing Hindenburg Park, he emphasized the social nature of the gatherings and stressed that the Bund was a tolerated group. The park served as a district site for Camp Sutter, a youth camp of the Jungenschaft movement. This organization was a community of youngsters modeled on the Hitler Youth. At the park, the Bund held dances and patriotic assemblies. These assemblies often featured speakers of other fascist organizations such as the Silver Shirts of William Dudley Pelly, the Khaki Shirts of General Art Smith and the White Shirts of Ralph H. Major Jr. Also present at the rallies were the Militant Christian Patriots. The Old Vienna restaurant, established in 1937 on Sunland Boulevard, was reportedly another hangout for the local Bund. There are a number of legends about the restaurant having secret passages and being used by German spies.

The bund's biggest rally at Hindenburg Park took place in 1939. A German cruiser was in town, and the crew was invited to join in the festivities. The main attraction was Fritz Kuhn, the American Fuhrer. During the speeches, a plane dive-bombed the crowd and dropped anti-Nazi handbills that read,

Hindenburg Park featured a huge bust of Paul Von Hindenburg, World War I German general and leader of Germany. The bust was located high in the southwest corner of the park, overlooking the grounds. It disappeared in the late '50s, when the county bought the park. *Fred Koegler.*

"Wanted for Kidnapping: Adolf Hitler…Indicted by World Opinion for Murder and Kidnapping with Intent to Kill." Fritz Kuhn had fought for Germany in World War I, after which he joined the Freikorp, a paramilitary group. In 1921, he joined the Nazi Party. In 1933, he joined the Bund and the following year became a U.S. citizen. He had been a petty criminal in Germany. While working for a Jewish friend, he stole $2,000. He claimed to have marched with Hitler in the 1923 Putsch. He was intelligent, had a fantastic ego and exaggerated his accomplishments. He loved food, drink and women. In 1939, he went to jail for four years after being convicted of grand larceny, forgery and embezzling $14,000, some of which he spent on mistresses. These and other vices led to his downfall. After World War II, he lost his citizenship and was deported back to Germany.

The size of the Bund is often disputed. We know it had a minimum of 6,000 members and 100 local units. Membership estimates go as high as 100,000; however, 25,000 is probably more accurate. Between the years 1919 and 1933, 400,000 Germans immigrated to the United States. The Bund's goal was to unite all German Americans, but the group appealed only to a certain number of first-generation immigrants. It is estimated that two-thirds of its membership was made up of former criminals, draft dodgers and sexual psychopaths. The Bund was nearly a complete failure. (Its greatest success was filling Madison Square Garden in 1939 with 25,000 supporters for a celebration of George Washington's birthday.) The group found it difficult to grow beyond the immigrant German population that was having trouble adjusting to life in American. The Bund ended with trials in the 1940s. In 1942, nine Los Angeles Nazis were convicted of violating the Sedition Act. In 1944, thirty-four more Nazis were put on trial for treason. Today, California State University–Northridge houses a large collection of local Nazi materials.

TUNA CAMP: WORLD WAR II PRISON FOR ENEMY ALIENS

Starting in 1933, the Civilian Conservation Corps (CCC) was established to assign out-of-work young American boys to useful labor projects in exchange for wages. Across the United States, camps were established from which teams of workers completed mostly outdoor jobs such as road building, swamp drainage and forestry maintenance. Here in the Crescenta Valley, there were three such camps established, and from those camps crews fought brush fires, worked on flood control projects and built the fire roads we see in our hills today. Tuna Camp was located on the western end of the valley, exactly where the Verdugo Hills Golf Course is today. By the 1940s, as the nation once again lurched toward war, most of the young men in the CCC program had found employment in the defense plants. In early 1941, Tuna Camp was closed.

A birds-eye view of Tuna Camp looking south. The Verdugo Mountains are in the background. Today, this view would show the Verdugo Hills Golf Course driving range, with the 210 Freeway just beyond. *Merrill H. Scott family.*

On December 7, 1941, the Japanese attack on Pearl Harbor shocked America. Although it caught American civilians and the U.S. Navy off guard, elements of U.S. intelligence in California were very ready and swung into action immediately. The FBI began rounding up anyone who was even remotely suspected of having a tendency toward disloyalty or who had any connections, no matter how remote, to foreign powers that we would soon be in conflict with. The U.S. Immigration and Naturalization Service (INS)—essentially today's U.S. Border Patrol—did its part in this effort by establishing holding areas for all the non-U.S. citizens who were bound to get caught in the FBI's nets.

On December 8, the day after Pearl Harbor, the U.S. Department of Justice commandeered the former CCC camp known as Tuna Camp and began stringing barbed wire and setting up sentry stations and floodlights. It renamed the site the Tuna Canyon Detention Station. It was to be an armed camp, and interrogations would be conducted while soldiers patrolled the twelve-foot-tall, barbed-wire-fenced perimeters. A week later, on December 16, the camp received its first prisoners, mostly Japanese from fishing communities in San Pedro and the South Bay. By Christmas, the camp held ninety-five men.

Tuna Canyon Detention Station, still known informally as Tuna Camp, differed from internment camps like Manzanar in that it was specifically for noncitizens, whereas the other internment camps held all people of Japanese descent, even U.S. citizens. (Because of restrictive immigration policies, Asians born outside of the United States were not eligible for citizenship even if they had lived here their entire lives.)

If individuals of Japanese descent maintained any connection at all to their culture or their native country, they were considered suspect. Many of the suspects rounded up for Tuna Camp were Japanese language instructors, photographers, martial arts practitioners and even radio enthusiasts. Any noncitizen in the Japanese American community who showed leadership abilities, such as heads of chambers of commerce or religious leaders, was arrested. Anyone who could form or participate in a "fifth column" was taken out of circulation.

These policies seem harsh by today's standards, but when one looks back on the newspapers from the months just after Pearl Harbor, we realize that the West Coast was in full panic mode. News articles carried headlines such as "Water Hoarded in Japanese Homes" and "Pupils Taught Hirohito Divine." The papers printed tales of Japanese fishermen being caught signaling Japanese submarines and secret stashes of binoculars, cameras and short-wave radios being found in Japanese American homes. Californians, it seems, expected attack by sea from Japan, and they were suspicious that Japanese Americans—or any citizens of the Axis nations—would rise up to help the invasion.

And so Tuna Camp became a first stop for those of Japanese, German or Italian descent who didn't have or couldn't prove U.S. citizenship. They were processed, sorted and interrogated at Tuna Camp and then sent on to larger federal prisons inland, to internment camps or, occasionally, as in the case of a few lucky Europeans, released. A report issued from Tuna Camp in 1942 stated that from December 16, 1941, to May 25, 1942, 1,378 of the 1,490 Japanese males processed at the camp were transferred to federal prisons in Fort Missoula, Fort Lincoln and Santa Fe. In addition, 36 were released, presumably to join their families in internment camps, and 76 were still in custody. Other reports record German and Italian citizens being picked

This is a view of the western edge of Tuna Camp that shows prisoners playing horseshoes. Note the tall fence topped with barbed wire and the guard tower overlooking the prisoners. On the hillside in the background is another guard tower that overlooks the entire camp. *Merrill H. Scott family.*

up on curfew violations (8:00 p.m.) and interrogated. Afterward, they were either sent to prison or released.

Conditions in the camp were good by wartime standards, particularly to a population that was used to Depression-era privations. There were seven barracks available to house up to three hundred prisoners, along with several other buildings, a mess hall, an infirmary and shops and offices. The prisoners were allowed free range of the enclosure, exercise was encouraged and some prisoners, despite their generally short stays, planted gardens or tidied up the compound. But they were still prisoners, and no amount of free range or exercise could dull the pain and humiliation of arrest and separation from their families. Those families were often in the process of being marched off to internment camps without their fathers or grandfathers, who had been left behind the barbed wire of Tuna Camp.

Diasho Tana, who immigrated to the United States in 1928 and was arrested in March 1942 in Santa Barbara because he was a Buddhist priest, wrote about receiving visitors at Tuna Camp:

> *We are prohibited to go within ten feet of the fence, and it is most painful to be cut off from the outside world. So many families were excited and came here. After thirty minutes of the visit I can see people's eyes filled with tears* [visits were limited to thirty minutes]. *Internees are waving their hands goodbye as the visitors go to the distant parking lot. What can they talk about through the iron fence for thirty minutes? And those who cannot speak English must talk through someone who can understand Japanese* [communication through the fence was limited to English].

The head of the camp, an INS civilian named Merrill Scott, had a high opinion of the Japanese, Germans, Italians, South Americans and Poles who made up the prisoner population. He told a minister who visited Tuna Camp:

> *I could open this camp at any time and say, "Gentlemen, you may go home to your wives and your families. Come back tomorrow evening by five o'clock." They'd go home and have a good time, and they'd all get back by five o'clock, and wouldn't do any damage while they were out. But I have to have Sarge, an old retired soldier, with a pistol at the gate, and they insisted on building towers with a fellow with a gun on top for these perfectly loyal Americans.*

It sounds like a heartless and unfair situation—and it was—but we must see it through the eyes of the time. One longtime local told me that "it was for their own good," as they needed protection from an inflamed American population. And indeed there were stories of local assaults on Asians. We can't forget the Spencer Tracy movie *Bad Day at Black Rock*, in which a Japanese American man, whose son died fighting heroically on the battlefields of Italy, is murdered by small-town vigilantes. That was the mood of America at that time.

But one American saw the injustice and acted on it. Herbert Nicholson, a retired Quaker missionary living in Pasadena, followed his Japanese friends to the internment camps, starting with Tuna Camp, and offered to relay messages, funds and packages between separated friends and families. He

Interior view of the guard station, with "Sarge," an armed guard, at his post. *Merrill H. Scott family.*

started a free trucking service in and out of Los Angeles to internment camps in Manzanar, Poston and Gila River carrying pets, large valuables, important papers, keys to safe-deposit boxes and even the ashes of deceased loved ones. Nicholson was a frequent visitor to Tuna Camp.

Nicholson's wife performed a service of her own for the incarcerated Japanese. Hillcrest Sanitarium, a large sanitarium located in La Crescenta at the top of Lowell Avenue, had been commandeered by the government at the beginning of the war. It was used to treat the Japanese American internees from the western states who had been diagnosed with tuberculosis. Mrs. Nicholson spent much of her time with these dying patients. The Nicholsons' story is told in a now out-of-print book from the '70s titled *Valiant Odyssey: Herbert Nicholson In and Out of America's Concentration Camps* by Weglyn and Mitson.

Tuna Camp and the Medal of Honor

Tuna Camp has a connection to our nation's highest military honor, the Congressional Medal of Honor. Several years ago, the Little Landers Historical Society in Tujunga, which has done the lion's share of research on the history of Tuna Camp, circulated a *Los Angeles Herald-Examiner* photo of a group of Japanese nationals being processed into Tuna Camp in 1942. In a weird twist of fate, it was seen by Torrance resident Diane Tanouye, whose parents had been sent to the internment camps and whose grandfather had been arrested by the FBI. When Diane first saw the photo, she was stunned. She looked into the eyes of a disheveled, humiliated older man at the back of the lineup of arrestees in the photo and said breathlessly, "That's my grandfather!"

The story she had heard as a child of her grandfather being brutally hustled away in the middle of the night by FBI agents began to crystallize for her. Nikuma Tanouye had been a proud, dignified man, a master of the martial art of Kendo and the father of five sons. The Old World concept of family honor was very strong in Japanese American families, and the idea that the family's door had been kicked in during a midnight raid and that the patriarch of the family had been arrested brought great shame to the family name. Nikuma's eldest son, Ted, now faced a dilemma: would he stay with the leaderless family as they went into the internment camps, or would he bring honor back to his family's name by serving his country? He chose the latter and was subsequently inducted into the famous all–Japanese American army unit the 442nd Infantry Regiment.

The 442nd was filled with young men with something to prove. Like Ted, many of them came from families whose patriotism had been called into question. The soldiers were motivated to great bravery by the desire to prove their detractors wrong, and the 442nd became one of the most decorated regiments in the U.S. armed forces, racking up twenty-one Medals of Honor in the waning years of World War II. Ted must have thought often of his father's humiliation, of his sad face framed in the barbed wire of Tuna Camp, of his family's shame.

Perhaps this image was in his mind when he led the assault on Hill 140, a strategic hilltop in Italy held by interlocking German machine gun positions. American units had been pinned down for days at the bottom of the hill. Ted crawled forward alone, taking out three enemy positions single-handedly. Now wounded in his left arm, he crawled back

Japanese American heads of households and community leaders in the Los Angeles area were dragged from their homes and taken to Tuna Camp while their families were hustled off to internment camps. Here, a group of men are searched after being arrested in the middle of the night. At the end of the line is Nikuma Tanouye. His crime? He was a martial arts teacher. *Little Landers Historical Society*.

for more ammo. He struck out alone again for the top of the hill, taking three more enemy strongholds, until he reached the top and called up his platoon. Not until his men's position was secured did he get his arm treated. Four weeks later, he returned to the front lines, where he was killed by a land mine.

The contributions of the 442nd and men like Ted Tanouye changed America's mind about the way it had treated Japanese Americans. With the posthumous award of the Medal of Honor to the Tanouye family, honor was returned to their family name—honor that had been stripped from them at Tuna Camp in our own Crescenta Valley.

THE BIZARRE INTERNATIONAL PRISONERS OF TUNA CAMP

Wartime America made some decisions about whom its enemies were that today we would think unfair and arbitrary. With the 1942 decision to remove those of Japanese ancestry from strategic areas of the West Coast also came the decision to protect the Panama Canal from those same perceived threats. The United States made an agreement with thirteen South American countries to "send us your Japanese"—both to remove them from the canal zone and also to provide a pool of "Japanese POWs" for prisoner exchanges with Japan. Peru, in particular, had a large and prosperous population of Japanese immigrants, most of whom had been there since the 1800s. The government of Peru saw this as a chance to not only create goodwill with the powerful United States but also commandeer some land and lucrative businesses from successful Japanese Peruvian citizens. Several thousand Japanese Peruvians were grabbed from their homes without warning, hustled onto the dark holds of U.S.-bound cargo ships and stripped of their passports. The shiploads of confused Peruvians reaching ports in Texas and San Pedro were greeted as illegal aliens and immediately incarcerated, many of them in Tuna Camp.

These were truly men without a country, some speaking only Spanish and with no local contacts, completely at the mercy of their captors. Tuna Camp in the Crescenta Valley proved a welcome respite for many of them after being confined in the holds of northbound ships. They were fed well and given a chance to get their bearings. They were next shuffled off to a federal prison at Crystal City, Texas, for the duration. During the war, about eight hundred of these Peruvian Japanese were indeed exchanged for American POWs. The rest of this "lost tribe" was left there in Texas when the war ended.

Their future was murky at this point. They had no ties to the United States. Most of those who tried to return to South America found they had been disowned and weren't allowed back in. About one thousand were allowed to go to Japan, where they might have had distant relatives. Some of them, bewildered and with nowhere else to go, simply stayed where they were in the Texas prison as late as 1948. The only cohesive group of them left today springs from a group of three hundred who were granted the legal right to stay in the United States when a large produce farm in rural New Jersey needed cheap farm labor and agreed to take them on. These odd pawns of World War II formed a small community that still survives today in Seabrook, New Jersey, where they have a small museum dedicated to their strange history.

Another odd story involving Tuna Camp is the undocumented tale of a group of Polish women and children who escaped the Nazi slave labor camps in occupied Poland and made their way on foot through war-torn Europe. They walked all the way to India, where they hitchhiked on a ship bound for Los Angeles and ended up at Tuna Camp. We have nothing on this group other than second-hand info, but for future writers and researchers out there, this is a tale worthy of a novel or screenplay!

There were even a few German citizens who processed through Tuna Camp as well. Many of them were unfortunates just caught on the wrong side of the Atlantic, but a few were more sinister. There had been an active American Nazi Party, called the Bund, in Los Angeles before the war. It had held a few pro-Nazi rallies in the '30s at Hindenburg Park, now Crescenta Valley Park. Ironically, some of those rally organizers, who saw themselves as a "fifth column" for Germany, now found themselves incarcerated in Tuna Camp, just blocks from their former rally site. They indeed had concrete plans for their takeover that can still be visited today. The ruins of "Murphy Ranch," their planned fortified headquarters in the Santa Monica Mountains, are now a Los Angeles City Park in Rustic Canyon.

TUNA CAMP AND CHARLIE CHAPLIN'S CHAUFFEUR

One Japanese man who spent time at Tuna Camp on a charge of spying was Toriachi Kono, Charlie Chaplin's right-hand man during his biggest years of stardom and, later, a champion for the rights of Japanese American internees.

Young Kono, born in Japan in 1885, had a wild streak, and his angry father sent him to America to finish his education. In 1916, he drifted to Los Angeles, where he answered a newspaper ad for a chauffeur. His new employer was rising star Charlie Chaplin. The two hit it off, and Kono soon became more than Chaplin's driver—he became his personal assistant and managed all the star's affairs. Chaplin called him "my man Friday."

An example of their strong connection was the legendary story behind the release of one of Chaplin's biggest films, *The Kid*. Chaplin had just finished filming, but his estranged wife's lawyers were going to seize the film reels as assets. In some accounts, Chaplin and Kono took unedited reels of film and fled in the middle of the night, driving east until they ran out of gas. At that point, they hopped a train and eventually holed up incognito in a hotel room in Utah, where they edited *The Kid* to its final version, bringing it back to Hollywood a masterpiece.

For seventeen years, Kono was Chaplin's gatekeeper. Hollywood stars, heads of state and even Chaplin's family had to go through Kono to reach him. Kono was an extra in many of Chaplin's films and used his influence to help secure a rising Japanese filmmaker tutelage under Chaplin. In 1932, Chaplin and Kono visited Japan, where Chaplin was the target of a failed assassination attempt meant to spark war with the United States.

But in 1933, Kono met his match in the form of Chaplin's newest love interest, Paulette Goddard. Goddard was jealous of Kono's influence over Chaplin, and vice-versa. The tension between the two men caused by Goddard was too great, and Chaplin and Kono ended their relationship in 1934. Kono then became the head of the Japanese arm of United Artists and spent time in Japan, where he was possibly courted by the Japanese military for info on the United States.

On June 8, 1941, Kono and a Japanese naval officer were swept up in an espionage arrest in Los Angeles. Kono was never charged with anything, and the allegations were dropped. However, on December 8 of that same year, Kono was re-arrested, along with many other Japanese or Japanese Americans of importance. When Tuna Camp opened that year, Kono was probably one of its first prisoners. Here we can assume he was interrogated for several weeks by the FBI about his role in the espionage case. Undoubtedly, he stood under the oaks of Tuna Camp—the same oaks that cover Verdugo Hills Golf Course today—gazing at the green Verdugo Mountains and the rugged San Gabriels and pondering his rise and fall here in Los Angeles. Sadly, no help was ever offered by Chaplin.

After Tuna Camp, Kono bounced around to various federal prisons in Montana, New Mexico, Texas, Idaho and New Jersey for the duration of the war. The end of the war came and went, but Kono was still incarcerated, seemingly forgotten for two years. He was finally released in 1947 with the help of a civil rights attorney. On his release, Kono returned to Los Angeles and dedicated the rest of his life to restoring the rights of Japanese Americans. He worked with the Tule Lake Defense Team in downtown Los Angeles's Little Tokyo to restore citizenship to 4,700 Japanese Americans who, during internment, had been coerced into renouncing their citizenship. He was successful at this in 1954 and then traveled to Japan to help the many Japanese American citizens there who had been deported from the United States. His work is well known in the Japanese-American community. Kono died in 1971. The story of Toriachi Kono, Charlie Chaplin's right-hand man and accused spy, is yet another fascinating chapter in the saga of Tuna Camp.

TUNA CAMP CLOSES

By the end of 1942, the need for Tuna Camp had passed, as all enemy aliens in the Los Angeles area had been rounded up. In all, upward of 2,500 prisoners had been processed through the camp. The commander of the camp was transferred to a federal prison in Montana, and in 1943, Tuna Camp was closed. After the war, the intact facility was used for a decade or so as a county "reform school" for young boys. But in 1960, the site was purchased by a group of investors for development as a golf course. The buildings were demolished, and all traces of Tuna Camp were obliterated.

Currently, the land is up for redevelopment as a large housing tract. In 2013, the Los Angeles City Council declared the site a Los Angeles City Historical Monument. Los Angeles city councilman Richard Alarcon stated, "The Tuna Canyon Detention Station is an important piece of our history in the Northeast San Fernando Valley and a reminder of some of our darkest times as a community, nation and world. Declaring the Tuna Canyon Detention Station as a Historic Cultural Monument allows us to protect this important piece of our history and gives us the opportunity to continue to learn from our past mistakes and preserve this lesson for generations to come."

Chapter 5
Oddballs and Freaks

The Lamppost Swastikas of Montrose

Retired Rosemont Middle School history teacher Lynn McGinnis related recently that while he was walking in the Montrose area, he came upon a family gathered around a streetlight, one of them crouched down examining the base of the lamppost. Lynn said he knew immediately what was going on, as it's an issue that gets ugly in Montrose and Glendale about every four to five years. He approached the group and heard exactly what he was expecting to hear: "There are Nazi symbols on this lamppost!"

This oft-repeated scenario has been a headache for the city of Glendale for several decades, most famously in the mid-'90s, when the Jewish Defense League threatened Glendale with a lawsuit, demanding the lamppost symbols be removed. The lamppost swastika symbols—which are actually reversed and turned forty-five degrees from the Nazi logo—are in a two-inch-high band running around the base of most of the lampposts in Glendale. The decorative swastikas were a popular design element in the 1920s, when the lampposts were purchased and installed in huge quantities not only in Glendale but across the nation. This was many years before the swastika became identified with Nazi Germany.

Here is one of the famous "swastika lampposts" of Glendale, this one located at the intersection of Broadview and Market Street in Montrose. Despite the fact that the lampposts were installed in the 1920s, and that this swastika symbol is reversed from the infamous Nazi icon, these lampposts are regularly the subject of controversy. *Photo by Mike Lawler.*

The swastika as a symbol is over three thousand years old, its name deriving from a Sanskrit word literally meaning "well-being." The swastika, in both clockwise and counter-clockwise form, is found historically in almost all major cultures as a symbol of goodness in forms such as good luck charms, decorations and even religious icons with auspicious meaning. It's unfortunate that it is most remembered today for its relatively brief usage as a symbol of evil.

The city of Glendale has dealt with the swastika lampposts in various ways over the years. Schemes to grind off the logos or cover them with metal bands have been considered. For a while, when a pole needed to be replaced because of damage, the city put an expensive and mismatched modern pole in its place, bringing even more complaints from neighbors. More galling is the fact that the city owns vast quantities of old spare swastika posts, stored in maintenance yards and ready for placement, but is hesitant to use them.

Crescenta Valley resident John Drayman has an interesting story about swastika lampposts in Montrose. A few years ago, he led the efforts to get the historic old streetlights put back on Honolulu like they had been in the '20s and '30s. He knew that the city had swastika posts that could be restored, and so he assumed he'd have to deal with the inevitable hysterics. But when examining old photos of the streetlights on Honolulu, he saw that the old posts there didn't have the swastikas on them. He realized that in the mid-'20s, when the swastika lampposts were being put in all throughout Glendale, Glendale's northern city limit was Broadview, one block below Honolulu. Honolulu itself was unincorporated, and it wasn't annexed by Glendale until the '50s. He confirmed that the county had used a different supplier and found that the manufacturer for the old Honolulu lampposts, Union Metal in Ohio, still existed. When he contacted the company, he found it miraculously still owned the original wooden molds that had been custom-made for Montrose in the '20s. That fact lowered the cost of newly manufactured "old" lampposts to nearly the cost of restoring the city-owned swastika posts. Not only that, but they were more authentic, plus there would be no controversy! Those are the lampposts one sees on Honolulu today.

Next time you're out for a stroll in the Montrose Shopping Park, take a detour one block south to Broadview and check out the base of one of the lampposts there. When you first see the swastikas, it is admittedly a little bit of a shock. We've become so overly sensitized to the Nazi symbol that any swastika, no matter its orientation or angle, disturbs us. But remember that you know its history, and have a little chuckle to yourself as you think of the reactions of those who don't.

Local Alien Abduction Story

One of the earliest modern stories of extraterrestrial abductions came out of our own nearby Big Tujunga Canyon. These abductions, which began in 1953, predate the more famous Betty and Barney Hill abductions of 1961 but weren't publicized until 1980 with the publication of *The Tujunga Canyon Contacts* by Ann Druffel and D. Scott Rogo. Whether you believe in the whole UFO phenomenon or not, this book is fun to read, as most of the incidents in the book took place locally.

The book details the stories of several female abductees, starting with the story of two young women sharing an isolated cabin in Big Tujunga Canyon on March 22, 1953. In the middle of the night, the two women were awakened by a very bright light that seemed to surround the cabin. Time seemed to stand still until they were finally able to break their trance and flee. As they ran, one of the women spotted the filmy apparition of a longhaired man. Later on, hypnotists delved into the memories of these women, and those hypnotic regressions unlocked stories of what had happened during that trance-like period. Tales emerged of being taken onto an alien craft and undergoing medical examinations by large-headed, grey-skinned humanoid creatures. The women also reported further visits from the alien entities in subsequent years.

Four other cases involving alien contact with women in the Tujunga area are studied in the book, ranging from the original 1953 event up into the '70s, with more fantastic tales of entities moving through solid walls and the abductees being floated into waiting spaceships. One of the women even reported being given a cancer cure by the aliens. In most of these cases, the abductees were visited repeatedly.

One chapter is titled "The Tujunga UFO Milieu." This portion of the book reports the many strange doings over the years in and around Big Tujunga Canyon. Other strange sightings reported in the canyon included soundless black helicopters, daylight flying discs and misty grey figures called "light people" being seen by schoolchildren on camping trips. In fact, the entire area around Tujunga Canyon is considered by ufologists to be a "window" area for UFO phenomenon.

The later portion of the book details the various abduction defense techniques that these women developed over their many years of contacts with the extraterrestrials. Most involved mental strength through prayer, mantras or other such mind-mastering tricks to ward off unwanted contact

The Tujunga Canyon Contacts, written by Ann Druffel and D. Scott Rogo and published in 1980, covered one of the first of the many alien abduction stories to emerge in the last half of the twentieth century. This one took place in 1953 in our own backyard! *Photo by Mike Lawler.*

with these aliens. In fact, author Ann Druffel expanded this portion of her study of these cases into a subsequent book entitled *How to Defend Yourself Against Alien Abductions*. So if the first book gets you worried about living so close to a hotbed of alien abduction, her second book will calm your fears.

But Tujunga isn't the only Foothill community to have "close encounters." A 1955 article in the old *Crescenta Valley Ledger* newspaper is titled "Deputy Sheriffs See Flying Discs." Three sheriffs from the Montrose Sheriff's Station watched several flying saucers maneuvering over La Cañada and Flintridge in the late afternoon. According to the deputies, for forty-five minutes, they watched as the strange craft hovered, bunched, formed into figures and flew over each other. Other calls were received by the sheriff's station reporting the strange sight. In keeping with the Cold War mindset of that era, a call was made to Norton Air Force Base, and fighter jets were scrambled. Just before the jets arrived over Crescenta Valley, the objects merged into one and disappeared from view. The three deputies would not retract their statements.

Rockets and Satanists

Jet Propulsion Laboratory (JPL), located in La Cañada, is a federally funded research and development center and also a NASA field center. JPL is managed by the nearby California Institute of Technology (Caltech). The laboratory's primary function is the construction and operation of robotic planetary spacecraft. It is also responsible for operating NASA's deep space network. JPL traces its beginnings to the Guggenheim Aeronautical Laboratory at Caltech, where the first set of rocket experiments were carried out. Caltech graduate students Frank Malina, Weld Arnold, Apollo M.O. Smith and Tsien Hsue-Shen, along with Jack Parsons and Edward S. Forman, were behind these initial experiments. These men became known as the "Suicide Squad" because of their casual use of highly explosive rocket fuel. The first test took place in the Arroyo Seco near the Devil's Gate Dam. In 1941, the military became interested in their experiments. The Suicide Squad was able to assist the army in producing Jet Assisted Take Off (JATO) rockets. In 1943, Malina, Parsons and Forman established the Aerojet Corporation to manufacture JATO motors. In November of that same year, JPL became an army facility operated under contract by Caltech. America officially entered the Space Age in 1958. Since then, JPL has led the world in exploring our solar system. It has produced such satellites as Mariner, Viking, Magellan, Voyager, Galileo, Mars Pathfinder, Mars Odyssey and, more recently, the Spirit and Opportunity rovers. Today, the laboratory, located on the eastern edge of La Cañada Flintridge, has over four thousand employees and is the valley's largest employer.

The aforementioned is a straight, bare-bones account of the founding and history of JPL. However, the facility has another, much more colorful history. That history is well covered in the books *Strange Angel* by George

In February 1942, there were only a few primitive shacks and rocket motor test pits on the edge of the Arroyo Seco, where the modern Jet Propulsion Laboratory now stands. *www.jpl.nasa.gov.*

Pendle, which is a biography of Marvel Whiteside Parsons, and *Going Clear* by Lawrence Wright. Marvel Whiteside Parsons, who preferred to be called John, was one of the founders of JPL. His story is one that really goes to the dark side.

Parsons was a self-educated man, a man of science and a self-described magician/wizard. It is fascinating that a man of science could also believe in his ability to transcend the physical laws of nature. Parsons was born into wealth and was considered a spoiled child. He had few friends and led a rich fantasy life. He read about King Arthur, the Arabian Knights and Greek and Norse mythology, as well as the stories of H.P. Lovecraft, Jules Verne, H.G. Wells and Edgar Allan Poe. Parsons had his first mystical experience late in the 1920s when he tried to invoke the devil. He apparently was successful enough to terrify himself. Parsons's formal education was limited. He attended John Muir High School in Pasadena, graduated from University High and dropped out of Pasadena City College after one term. He began to experiment with rockets in the 1920s, when he also started correspondence with Werner von Braun. In the 1930s, he collaborated with Caltech students in a wide range of rocket experiments. Due to the dangerous and careless conduct of their experiments, they were banished to the Arroyo Seco, where they annoyed the neighbors with loud noises and bad smells. In April 1936, the U.S. Army became interested in their work and began to finance the program. World War II would provide the impetus for the expansion of JPL. The staff increased from eighty-five in 1943 to over four hundred by the end of the war. The army's interest led to increased bureaucracy, conformity and emphasis on academic credentials. All of these became obstacles to the un-credentialed, freewheeling Parsons. JPL grew away from Parsons, who no longer fit in. As Parsons's scientific career went into decline, he became more interested in and obsessed with mystical and religious activities. This increased interest further alienated him from the scientific community. In 1944, he quit JPL to pursue magic full time. He said that this was to be his real life's work.

Parsons was a follower of Aleister Crowley, who billed himself as the wickedest man alive and called himself the "Great Beast." According to Crowley, the full text of the law was "do what thou wilt." Crowley certainly lived his faith. He broke all moral codes, and his behavior was unbounded. He was an alcoholic, drug addict and sexual connoisseur. He believed that sexual ecstasy could bring one to a higher plane of consciousness. Crowley believed that there were ten levels of attainment. The secrets of sex would be revealed when you attained level nine. Parsons joined Ordo Templi Orientis, a cult that believed in hidden knowledge, demons, unrestrained sex, reincarnation and hedonism. Parsons ran his church from a mansion on South Orange Grove Avenue in Pasadena. This house at one time had entertained Teddy Roosevelt, John Muir and Albert Einstein. Parsons's mansion contained an interesting group of people, including an opera singer, astrologists, an ex-convict and the famous creator of Scientology, L. Ron Hubbard, who moved into the mansion after World War II. Hubbard was charming and witty and proved to be irresistible to women. Parsons and Hubbard became rivals for the affections of Parsons's wife, Helen. In this duel of personalities, Parsons was defeated. To replace his lost love, he decided to engage in a magical process to replace her. What followed was two weeks of intense rituals. Aided by Hubbard, the process was successful and produced Marjorie Cameron, Parsons's love goddess. Hubbard and Parsons's contentious friendship ended because of a disagreement over a business deal. It all came to an end for Parsons at 5:08 p.m. on June 17, 1952.

Parsons worked for Bermite Powder Company in Saugus. The company manufactured pyrotechnics. Parsons was mixing a rush order and carelessly dropped the explosive mixture. The blast caused him horrendous injuries, and he died forty-five minutes later. His mother, after learning of his death, rushed home and took her own life.

Mommy Dearest

If you remember the film *Mommy Dearest*, you may not have realized that the school where Joan Crawford's daughter Christina was sent to "shape up" was Flintridge Sacred Heart Academy in La Cañada. The school is pictured in the film as a very dark place. Many of the school's supporters would disagree with that characterization. Also, the characterization of Joan

Christina Crawford, daughter of Joan Crawford, attended Sacred Heart Academy, a prestigious Catholic girls' school in Flintridge, in the late 1950s. She later remembered it as a positive experience in her life. *Photo by Mike Lawler.*

Crawford's character in the movie and in the book is highly controversial. However, Flintridge Sacred Heart Academy is not the only contact our community has had with the Crawfords. In 1955, the *Ledger* printed a story on Christopher Crawford, the adopted son of Joan Crawford. He had been picked up by sheriff's deputies at Foothill Boulevard and Rosemont Avenue after having run away from the Mount Lowe Military Academy. He was returned to the academy without incident.

THE HOG FARM

One of the many widespread social experiments of the 1960s was the commune. Communes were composed of people who agreed to work and live together—to share their property, minds and bodies. The Hog Farm in Sunland-Tujunga is one of the best-known communes, and it's certainly is one of the most successful. It is still doing good work to this day.

In 1965, Hugh Romney, later to become "Wavy Gravy," and his wife, Bonnie Jean, were living in a one-room cabin in Sunland before being evicted. Fortunately, a neighbor, "Old Saul," had a stroke and needed help slopping his hogs up in Big Tujunga Canyon. Thus, the Hog Farm was born. The Hog Farm sat on a low hill that, today, overlooks a new golf course in the Tujunga Wash. It is an isolated and peaceful place—a place that would appeal to hippies. One day in the mid-'60s, Charlie Manson visited the Hog Farm. He drove up to the farm in his all-black tour bus. Shirley Lake, one of the Hog Farm members, would lose her daughter Diane to the Manson Family. Manson tried to seduce Bonnie Jean. He was apparently planning to push Hugh Romney out and take over as leader at the Hog Farm. To rid the Hog Farm of Manson and his bad vibes, Romney surrounded the bus with his supporters. They began a chant. Manson's supporters tried to get them to stop—they said that Manson was gasping for breath. Manson emerged from the bus holding his throat and choking. His female followers believed that the chant was killing Manson. To counter Romney, Manson's followers began a chant of their own. Eventually, Romney convinced Manson to leave. The following year, Romney changed his name to "Wavy Gravy" and became famous as the emcee at the Woodstock Music Festival. At Woodstock, he was also the director of security and the head of the soup kitchen. Manson went on to other kinds of fame.

In the earliest days of the hippie movement, a commune called the Hog Farm was located on the edge of Big Tujunga Canyon. Charlie Manson wanted this to be his base of operations but was rebuffed by the owner. Here we see the residents gathered for a town meeting, circa 1967–68. Avante Garde *magazine, 1968.*

Today, the Hog Farm land belongs to the Hallelujah Church. The main building is still intact, but the area is no longer open to the public. The Hog Farm is still active in Berkeley, California, and eight other locations around the nation.

Chapter 6
Cons and Swindles

Frank Flint

Frank Flint had all the advantages. He was intelligent, movie-star handsome and a gifted ladies' man. He was a well-known lover, and he was not always careful about where he sought affection. He was once shot by a jealous husband. He was the assistant U.S. district attorney from 1892 to 1893, a Superior Court judge from 1896 to 1897 and a Los Angeles County district attorney from 1897 to 1901. He was also a U.S. senator, a deputy marshal, a banker and a real estate speculator. Frank and his brother arrived in Los Angeles via San Francisco in 1888. They came to make their fortune in real estate. The land boom of 1888 was one of those periodic land frenzies that occurred in California. At the peak of the boom, there were twelve thousand realtors in Los Angeles alone. There were no laws regulating land speculation, and anything and everything was done to sell land. Theatrical stars, Spanish dancers and yacht races were all used to promote the sale of land. The Santa Fe Railroad brought people in from the East for as little as one dollar. People bought land at Eagle Rock at noon and sold it for double the price at 5:00 p.m. Frank made his fortune before the bubble burst. Frank Flint was elected to the U.S. Senate by the California legislature. He served one term, from 1905 to 1911. He was a

This is a 1920s postcard view of the clubhouse of the Flintridge Country Club and its world-class golf course. The 210 Freeway took much of the golf course, and this beautiful Mission-style building was incorporated into St. Francis High School. *Glendale Public Library*.

Frank Flint's crowning achievement was to be this grand hotel overlooking his mansion-filled Flintridge subdivision, seen here under construction in 1927. Despite its luxurious accommodations, the venture failed and the hotel was sold to the Catholic Church in 1931. Today, it is the Sacred Heart Academy, a Catholic girls' school. *Glendale Public Library*.

In addition to founding Flintridge, Frank Flint is also remembered for his role in the controversial politics of water for Los Angeles. As a U.S. Senator in 1905, his legislation made possible the confiscation of water from the Owens Valley, thus ensuring the growth of Los Angeles and the financial success of land developers like himself. He was honored with this fountain at Los Angeles City Hall in 1933. *Photo by Mike Lawler.*

creature of the Southern Pacific Railroad. During his time in Washington, he was on President Teddy Roosevelt's Panama Canal commission. He was a friend of Roosevelt's and was instrumental in securing Owens Valley water for Los Angeles.

At the turn of the century, Hiram Johnson was elected governor of California. He brought a strong progressive reform movement to the state. His campaign slogan was "Kick the Southern Pacific out of Politics." Frank, fearing defeat at the poles, decided not to run for reelection. He decided instead to develop a wealthy community as a suburb of Pasadena. Being an egotist, he named it after himself: Flintridge. He rode through the foothills and laid out twenty miles of riding trails. Those trails became the roads we know today as Inverness, Highland, Berkshire and Chevy Chase. The clubhouse for the golf course is today part of St. Francis High School. But the prize of Frank's holdings was the Flintridge Hotel, built in 1927. He poured his best efforts and $1 million into the hotel, which boasted a swimming pool, a bowling green, tennis courts and a nine-hole golf course. Located at the top of the highest peak in the San Rafael Hills, the hotel covered forty acres and had one hundred rooms but never had more than eleven guests at a time. Its expense and location worked against its success. It eventually failed and became a Biltmore hotel. Today, it is home to the Flintridge Sacred Heart Academy.

When the hotel failed, Frank and his brother were involved in what would be, for Los Angeles, the crime of the century. It was the Julian Oil Scandal, in which forty thousand investors lost over $150 million. In today's currency, that would be in excess of $1.5 billion. It was the little investors, not the large ones, who lost money, as they were guaranteed profits in the million-dollar pool. Frank was legal counsel for the deal. His brother Motley was charged with forgery, embezzlement and security violations but was never tried. The case led to Motley's murder in a Los Angeles courtroom. Frank was not charged, but his reputation was ruined. He had a nervous breakdown and took a sea cruise to regain his health. While on the cruise, however, he suffered a major heart attack and died. He was sixty-four years old. He is buried at Forest Lawn. Los Angeles City Hall has a statue and fountain dedicated to the memory of Frank Flint in recognition of his role in securing the Owens Valley water for Los Angeles. His name lives on in Flintridge, Flint Peak and Flint Canyon.

Harry F. Sinclair

Harry Ford Sinclair was born on July 6, 1876, in Wheeling, West Virginia. Sinclair's father was a pharmacist, and Harry planned on following in his father's footsteps after graduating from the University of Kansas in 1898. He inherited his father's business but soon realized that he had no interest in the drugstore and sold it. He invested in lumber, which eventually led to oil derricks and an interest in the oil industry. Oil made Harry a millionaire before his thirtieth birthday. His ambition grew in proportion to his wealth, and he decided that he would be bigger than John D. Rockefeller. Sinclair became a sportsman, successfully raising and racing horses. He also invested in the short-lived Federal Baseball League and was one of the few to actually make money in the league. He lived large, wagering hundreds of thousands of dollars at Arnold Rothstein's casino in Saratoga, Florida. Rothstein was the man accused of fixing the World Series in the Black Sox scandal. In 1918, Sinclair went to Russia to negotiate with Vladimir Lenin for access to Russian oil fields. When Sinclair returned to the United States, he found himself in the middle of the greatest scandal of the Harding administration. The Teapot Dome was a Wyoming oil field that had been made a U.S. Navy oil reserve. This was to ensure that in the event of future wars, the navy would have a guaranteed source of oil. Sinclair was accused of bribing the secretary of the interior, Albert B. Fall, with $233,000 in Liberty Bonds to gain access to Teapot Dome. The money was delivered to Fall's son-in-law via Sinclair's private railroad car. An additional $160,000 was contributed by Sinclair to the Republican National Committee under Will Hays. This is the same Will Hays who was later hired by Hollywood to clean up immorality in the movies. Fall was found guilty of accepting a bribe and went to jail for a year. Sinclair was tried but—incredibly—was found not guilty. Senator Gerald Nye noted that the verdict was "disgusting and discouraging… everybody in the United States knows that he is guilty." Fall found it difficult to believe he could be found guilty for receiving a bribe from Sinclair, when Sinclair was found innocent of offering the bribe in the first place. Sinclair did not get away unscathed, however. He had hired a detective agency to shadow the jurors, hoping to find one or more to bribe. He was convicted of contempt of court and spent six months in jail. During his time, he worked as the prison pharmacist and received other privileges, including being allowed to wear silk pajamas to bed. These, of course, were not prison issued. Upon leaving jail, he was totally unrepentant, claiming that he had been railroaded. Sinclair realized $100 million from Teapot Dome—I am

Harry Sinclair's spectacular mansion still stands on Alta Vista Drive in La Cañada. The house is ten thousand square feet and sits on two acres of landscaped grounds. Sinclair purchased it in the 1930s with some of the $100 million he realized from the Teapot Dome scandal. *Photo by Mike Lawler.*

sure he considered himself well compensated for his six months in jail. Sinclair continued to make money even during the Depression and World War II. In 1947, he liquidated his companies and retired to his home in La Cañada, where he died a wealthy man in November 1956.

Crescenta Valley's Oil Boom of 1927

In the 1920s, Los Angeles was in the grip of oil fever. Oil had always been a part of the natural landscape of Southern California. It had been used by the Indians to waterproof their boats and by the Spanish to seal their roofs. It wasn't until the 1890s that oil was extracted on a commercial scale, with Edward Doheny's first well near downtown Los Angeles. As the fuel industry shifted from coal to oil, the efforts to tap the huge oil reserves under the Los Angeles area intensified, and by 1923, a quarter of the world's oil was coming from Los Angeles.

During this oil boom, a real estate boom was happening as well, and the two began to overlap. Stories began to circulate about people like Orange County farmer Alphonso Bell, who, while digging a water well, struck oil and became a millionaire land developer. He named his community after himself: Bel Air. Soon every property owner in Los Angeles was convinced that oil could be found under even small suburban lots, and the real estate prices spiraled out of control based on speculation. Stocks in nonexistent wells were bought and sold, and any drilling derrick, producing or not, increased the value of a property. With this gold rush mentality, swindlers flourished, and in 1927, they visited our sleepy valley.

According to the local newspaper, a mass meeting held in the auditorium of La Crescenta Elementary School was attended by an overflow crowd. Every seat was taken—people were standing against the walls, pushing through doors and windows and trying to hear from the corridor outside. A "committee of local businessmen" (one real estate agent) had hired a "geologist" (a con man) to give a report on his discoveries of oil deposits in the area. He regaled the crowd with stories of oil seepage found at the top of New York Avenue, at a spot in Sparr Heights and at the base of the Verdugo Mountains near today's Crescenta Valley Park. Reports also highlighted indications of oil found on Collins Hill (at the intersection of Ocean View and the 210 Freeway). Getting into the spirit, Charles Bowden, who had just developed Indian Springs Resort in Montrose, reported hitting oil at eight feet while digging on his property on the northeast corner of Honolulu and La Crescenta.

This meeting had actually been organized by Montrose real estate agent Fred Anderson. Coincidentally, Anderson was also the head (and only member) of the "committee" investigating local oil possibilities. Anderson promised free maps that would show the extent of the massive pool of oil just beneath the surface of the valley. The geologist had reported that a gigantic stream of oil flowed from Newhall, where pumps were already producing, along the base of the San Gabriel Mountains and into a huge underground pool beneath the Crescenta Valley. Anderson warned that local properties where oil had just been discovered had already been taken off the market and were no longer for sale by their lucky owners. However, he related in the news article that he'd be happy to set up a private meeting with the geologist and anyone interested in buying or selling potential oil-bearing property.

It can be assumed by the lack of further news articles about oil that the "geologist" had disappeared. The "local businessmen" had made a tidy profit off the brief spike in local real estate prices, and embarrassed investors who had been taken in the deal had quietly dropped the whole matter.

At the same time, over on the Tujunga side, con artists actually set up a working derrick next to Foothill Boulevard near the Big Tujunga Wash. One old-timer who remembered the operation related that the derrick operated only on the weekends, when motorists out for a pleasant Sunday drive were likely to see it working. Presumably, shares in the well could be bought on the spot, and I'm sure investors were shocked to find the dry well abandoned several weeks later.

If you're interested in the possibility of oil beneath your property in the Crescenta Valley, you will be disappointed. There is no oil—just lots and lots of rocks.

ANGELO MOZILO AND COUNTRYWIDE FINANCIAL

High-interest loans for the poor and favorable loans for friends of Angelo Mozilo were the order of the day at Countrywide Financial. Angelo's friends included U.S. senators and cabinet members. Mozilo, the son of a butcher, co-founded Countrywide Financial in 1969 and eventually built it into the largest mortgage lender in the United States. Countrywide was not the first to offer exotic mortgages to credit-poor borrowers, but it did popularize them. *Time* magazine rated Angelo Mozilo as the number-one man responsible for the financial disaster of 2008. In June 2009, the Securities and Exchange Commission (SEC) accused Mozilo of fraud, charging that he had hid the risk of the company's loans from shareholders. While doing so, he made $140 million in profits from stock sales. The SEC quoted e-mails in which Mozilo described certain Countrywide loan products as "toxic" and "poison." This was three years before the term "toxic debt" entered the nation's vocabulary. "In the end, these former executives made deliberate decisions to mislead investors," said Robert Khozami, a federal prosecutor. Mozilo stated, "I have no regrets about how Countrywide was run." And why should he? He walked away with a total of $471 million dollars. Mozilo netted $139 million between November 2006 and August 2007—just before the housing bubble he had helped to create, burst. Mozilo lived across from the Oakmont

Glendale resident Angelo R. Mozilo was chairman of the board and CEO of troubled Countrywide Financial. Countrywide and Mozilo took much of the blame for the subprime mortgage crisis, which led to the financial meltdown of 2008. Mozilo, the son of a Bronx butcher, made millions before and after the crash. *www.marketoracle.co.uk.*

Country Club and was a contributor to St. Francis High School. He left Glendale for Thousand Oaks in 2012. He sold his 6,238-square-foot home for $2.9 million in 2013. The home had many custom features, including an infinity pool in the master suite. Mozilo left Countrywide after its sale to Bank of America in 2008. Bank of America pledged to pay $17 billion dollars to settle the disasters that Countrywide created. This included a $73 million dollar fine for Mozilo. As of December 2013, Countrywide's disaster has become Bank of America's $73 billion dollar mistake.

Chapter 7
Crime

Montrose Bank Robbery

In the summer of 1931, a lone African American man entered the Security First National Bank at the corner of Honolulu and Ocean View in Montrose (today Faye's). He approached the teller, placed a dime on the counter and quietly asked for two nickels. When the teller looked up, the robber had pulled his pistol and pointed it at the teller and a nearby secretary. The robber calmly told the teller to give him all the money in his drawer. The teller handed over $1,500, and the robber silently turned and left the bank. The robbery was so low key that the other tellers and the patrons didn't realize a robbery had taken place. The bandit escaped on foot and was never apprehended. It was later discovered that the same bank robber had entered the Crescenta-Canada Bank across the street (today Starbuck's) earlier that same day. He had asked for change for a quarter but apparently lost his nerve to go through with the robbery there.

THE GETTLE KIDNAPPING

It seems Montrose just couldn't stay out of the papers in the 1930s. Just four months after the great Montrose New Year's Flood, in a neighborhood still devastated by that flood, a nationally famous kidnapping took place, with spectacular "gangbusters" style arrests at the culmination.

William Gettle had made his fortune in oil in Los Angeles and lived the good life in a Beverly Hills mansion. On the night of May 9, 1934, Gettle, spectacularly fat at over five hundred pounds, was drinking with a friend. Two men dressed in bed sheets like ghosts burst in and forced Gettle into their car at gunpoint. They drove him to Montrose, where they had rented a small house at 4256 Rosemont Avenue (today's 210 Freeway overpass). He was tied and gagged in the bedroom of the house but otherwise treated well.

A ransom note was sent to Gettle's lawyer demanding $60,000, and another was sent to his wife demanding an additional $40,000. Gettle was held in the house for six days while the ransom was negotiated and police scrambled for clues. On May 15, the police finally broke the case, but the tale of the capture of the kidnappers varies widely in the various news sources. All were exciting, but we'll show our hometown bias by using the *Crescenta Valley Ledger*'s version.

According to the *Ledger*, after a ransom drop-off spot was settled on, a car carrying $60,000 in cash was dispatched. A lookout for the kidnappers spotted the police following the car and called police headquarters, telling the "coppers" to "lay off tailing the car." As the lookout talked, the police traced the call to a Los Angeles address. They raided the site and nabbed the caller, a woman. Police found in her pocket a business card from Nate Zimmer, a La Crescenta real estate agent who had his office at Rosemont and Foothill, where Foster's Donuts is located today. A quick call to Mr. Zimmer revealed that he had just rented a house on Rosemont to strangers to the valley.

By the evening of the fifteenth, the police felt they had the location of the kidnappers. This was before the days of police negotiators and psychologists, so a score of LAPD and local sheriff's cars converged on the house with sirens blaring. Police surrounded the house armed with machine guns and shotguns and crashed through the front door. Two of the kidnappers inside, a man and a woman, surrendered immediately, while another male kidnapper abandoned his accomplices and leaped out the back window. He miraculously evaded the surrounding police but was soon caught in Los Angeles.

After the Gettle kidnapping made national news, one local entrepreneur made money by giving tours of the house where the raid took place. This sign tacked on the back of a car on Foothill Boulevard directs the curious to the kidnapping site. *Glendale Public Library.*

William Gettle was released unharmed, and the ransom money was retained. In all, five kidnappers were arrested: three men and two women. If you think the police were quick to react, that was nothing compared to the swiftness of the court system. The three male kidnappers were brought straight from Montrose to a courtroom, where, in an amazing fourteen-minute court proceeding, they plea-bargained to get out of death penalty charges and were sentenced to life in prison with no parole. Within sixty hours of their arrest, the three men were behind bars in San Quentin. The women were tried and sent to a reformatory.

Sadly, the nightmare wasn't over for William Gettle. By June 1934, he had received two death threats against him for his testimony against the female kidnappers, and at Christmas, he was threatened with another kidnapping. The stress was too much for the family, and the following year, his invalid wife died at the young age of thirty-four. Gettle himself died just six years later at age fifty-four.

The Foothill Boulevard Riot

Cruising in cars became a standard part of life for American teens during the post–World War II boom. All across the United States, masses of teenagers were driving slowly up and down the main street of town, socializing, stopping for food, showing off their cars and occasionally racing each other. In Los Angeles, Van Nuys Boulevard in the San Fernando Valley was the mecca for cruising, as each Wednesday night, thousands of youths "cruised Van Nuys." The phenomenon peaked in the '70s, and the release of 1973's *American Graffiti*, a movie about cruising, cemented the concept in the minds of that generation as a rite of passage.

In the Crescenta Valley in the '70s, most teenagers considered La Crescenta dead and void of entertainment. Someone came up with the idea of establishing a Monday night cruise on Foothill Boulevard between La Cañada and Tujunga, and on May 18, 1975, the first Foothill Cruise Night was inaugurated. All went well for two successive Monday nights, but as Cruise Night gained in popularity, attracting bigger crowds, the police decided to tighten down.

On the night of June 1, there were approximately four hundred cruisers out on Foothill, and the first of several confrontations between the cruising teens and police occurred. The western turnaround spot was the Lucky's parking lot (now Albertson's) just west of Lowell. A crowd of youths had gathered there, and the LAPD and Glendale Police decided to roust them out. They closed Foothill at Lowell, routing traffic south down Lowell, while two police helicopters hovered over the Lucky's parking lot, demanding the crowd of teenagers disperse.

The indignant kids scattered through the neighborhoods but found their way back to Foothill. At this point, about two hundred now angry kids had reassembled on both sides of Foothill at the far eastern turnaround spot in La Canada, where Pier One Imports and Ross Dress-For-Less are today. It was now up to the Crescenta Valley Sheriffs, supported by California Highway Patrol and the Glendale Police Department, to break up this eastern end of the cruise circuit. They assembled at what is now Big Lots and moved east in force toward the crowd, where they found the kids had barricaded Foothill Boulevard. As the police cars entered the area, they were met with a barrage of rocks and bottles. One officer was hit, and several police cars had their windows broken out. The police waded into the crowd making arrests, and again the kids scattered.

It was now midnight, and most of the teens had had enough. There would be plenty of stories to tell the next day at Crescenta Valley High School. A few returned to the Lucky's parking lot in Tujunga, but for the most part, the night's excitement was over. In all, there had been seventeen arrests, with the charges ranging from loitering and reckless driving all the way up to narcotics possession. Along Foothill Boulevard, there had been a reported $20,000 in property and vehicle damage, including a tractor-trailer that had been partially dismantled and a motor home whose roof had been caved in by kids jumping on it.

The police vowed that this would never happen again and promised to have an army of officers out the next Monday night. Sheriff Peter Pitchess offered a stern "No more!" to the Monday night cruising. Of course, to the kids, this sounded like a challenge. Fliers were passed out at high schools as far away as Glendale and San Marino with the following message: "The pigs think they can stop you from cruising Foothill on Monday nights. Foothill is publicly owned property. You have the right to do what you want to do—so do it! Remember, there's safety in numbers." Other messages were less belligerent but still urged the kids to come out the next Monday. The local paper published a letter from a group of teenagers that read, "This town has been dead long enough and we need at least one night where we have something to do. Let's show them we can have fun cruising, and at the same time conduct ourselves maturely." Tensions increased the following week as determined teens urged youths from surrounding high schools to show up on June 8. Even some Los Angeles rock radio stations called on kids to attend the next cruise night. The police showed up with an army on June 8. The California Highway Patrol, Glendale Police Department, LAPD and local sheriff's office established three command posts along Foothill Boulevard and fielded eighty patrol cars, twenty motorcycles and two helicopters.

The stretch of Foothill from Lowell east was kept under relative control. For three hours, a solid line of flashing red lights marked the edges of Foothill Boulevard as police pulled over every car that moved. Any gatherings of teenagers were broken up—forty-five were arrested, and fifty citations were given out.

But on the LAPD end west of Lowell, things got out of hand. A crowd of over seven hundred youths was allowed to build up in the Lucky's parking lot. For two hours, the crowd sporadically threw rocks and bottles at police and spilled out onto Foothill, stopping traffic. The crowd briefly tried to overturn an unfortunate RTD bus trapped there but failed. The police repeatedly called for the crowd to disperse, but it continued to build, and at 10:00 p.m.,

Above: This Dodge van continued its cruise down Foothill Boulevard on the hook of a tow truck while its teenage owner spent the night in county jail. This scene took place on Foothill just east of Ramsdell. *Historical Society of the Crescenta Valley.*

Left: Many of the crowd that gathered at the Lucky's lot near Foothill and Lowell wanted to keep Cruise Night going by urging restraint from both the cruisers and the police. One side of this teenaged boy's sign read, "Let's keep it cool," while the other side read, "Leave us alone." *Historical Society of the Crescenta Valley.*

officers swept the sidewalk from west to east, arresting everyone they could catch before the crowd took off.

The arrests were dramatic—often an arresting officer was surrounded by teens screaming obscenities at him, raising tensions further. Cars were impounded and towed away by the score. News photographers had a field day, and dozens of photos of handcuffed kids struggling with police were printed. There's a great news photo of a line of twenty-five handcuffed teens in '70s attire linked together elbow to elbow with zip ties. One of the arrests turned potentially deadly as the arrestee wrestled with an officer and tried to grab his weapon. Two were arrested for possession of "Asiatic chain-handled weapons" (nunchakus?). The majority of arrests were for loitering and failure to disperse, with some narcotics possession and concealed weapons charges thrown into the mix. The kids had made use of CB radios to try to avoid or evade police. By 10:30 p.m., this cruise night was over.

Rob Ward graduated from Crescenta Valley High School in 1975 and is now retired and living in Orange County. He considers himself one of the organizers of Cruise Night. He remembers the following:

> *I know I was a vocal supporter of bringing a cruise night to our area since Wednesday night Van Nuys Boulevard cruising was so popular back then. I talked it up at CV High School and out to Van Nuys but can't remember much more than that on how it started and who was involved. I believe it was strong word of mouth.*
>
> *I had forgotten that we had two peaceful cruise nights before the third one where all hell broke loose. I remember on that third cruise night, myself and others were pulled over by the police for anything they could find. My "Dodge" sticker in the back window of my Challenger was actually legal as I had two outside mirrors on the car, but nevertheless they wrote me up for obstruction of view—a harmless fix-it ticket. I do recall that the two police officers that pulled me over were nice guys, and they both understood what we were trying to do. Not that it didn't happen, but I never saw any of the violence against the police that was reported in the newspapers, nor do I remember seeing any heavy-handed police activity. But the police definitely used different tactics that final night as I witnessed a lot of what I would call unnecessary hassling by the police earlier in the evening—which may have angered the crowd. I do remember watching the final act as the police lined up in the street east of Lowell with bullhorns blaring and then marching down Foothill arm in arm toward the La Crescenta side to break it up. I watched from a vantage point about a block up on the north side of Lowell.*

Given what I had witnessed that night—and I'm sure I missed a lot—I remember the description of kids getting way out of control, and the event being called a "riot" seemed weird to me. But again, I probably did not witness the events that may have triggered the response. I do recall that afterward I felt that the situation was overblown by the press to justify the crackdown and to prevent further cruise nights. As a "seasoned" adult today, I can fully understand their actions—especially the dangers of alcohol and drag racing and the thought that the whole cruise thing could get out of hand. But at that time, we were all very upset about how abruptly our seemingly harmless fun came to an end.

Another of the teenaged participants, Craig Baker, now middle-aged, recently wrote:

For better or worse, I was one of the people rocking the RTD bus. As I recall, the intent was only that—and people in the bus were laughing and seemed to be enjoying the excitement, albeit nervously. The bus driver was not happy, however. I don't recall any rock or bottle throwing, but I'm sure it happened. Rob Breiner and I had 50 bumper stickers printed that said, "Cruise Foothill—It's a Riot," but as soon as we stepped out the door of the printing shop in Montrose, we were confronted by two Glendale Police detectives who took the stickers (and Rob) away. He was questioned, threatened with a charge of inciting a riot and released the same day (he had paid for the stickers—I was just the driver).

Although every week had its crazy moments, the zenith of that brief period was, of course, the cruise on Monday, June 8th. In the beginning, the cruise was supposed to go back and forth from Jack in the Box in La Cañada to In-N-Out Burger just past Lowell. But fairly quickly, the shopping center parking lots at the top of the hill there became a focal point of activity and a place to gather. Hundreds and hundreds of people gathered near In-N-Out, and cars were taking turns peeling out of the Lucky's shopping center parking lot onto the eastbound lanes of Foothill. Someone had poured a lot of motor oil in the street so the spinning tires would generate huge clouds of smoke, and the cars were sometimes on the edge of control. Sometimes a driver would pull onto the patch of oil and stop, people would grab the door handles and hold the car back while the tires were spinning, burning the oil. Eventually, one of these cars did lose control, veered into the westbound lanes and collided with another car. The westbound driver sprang out of his car mad as hell, and the real mayhem began as the crowd then flooded

Some of the cruisers sought a peaceful solution to the conflict by meeting with local officials. Here we see a meeting between Captain Renfrow of the Crescenta Valley Sheriff's Station and two of the local cruisers, Dennis Taylor and Dave Ciccotelli. *Courtesy of the Historical Society of the Crescenta Valley.*

the street, completely closing Foothill Boulevard. A police helicopter circling above turned its spotlight on the crowd and hundreds of middle fingers were immediately raised at it in response. It felt like a cross between a rock concert and a scene out of the Book of Revelations. You knew it was going to end soon, with what might involve running.

We'd seen the LAPD setting up a command post at Mountain View Elementary School (in Tujunga) earlier in the evening, so we knew they had done a lot of pre-planning. Officers in riot gear had been assembling on Foothill just west of the crowd and began to move toward and into it. Police used bullhorns, indicated that the gathering had been declared an unlawful assembly, and ordered the crowd to disperse, broadcasting which streets we were to use to leave the area. It certainly seemed like it was a good time for me to leave, but I could not safely reach my truck through the approaching riot police. Everything was completely chaotic. I got very lucky and was able to jump into a friend's moving car just in time, and we left—headed for Jack in the Box, of course.

A mobile booking station for processing those arrested by LAPD had been set up at the command post at the school, and buses normally used to transport jail inmates were parked there as well. Booking photos of the more than 100 arrested that night were taken against an outside wall of a school building, and fingerprinting was done there as well.

My mom and a friend of hers (both 50-ish school nurses) made a point of getting a window booth facing east at Love's Restaurant (at the west end of the Lucky's shopping center) so that they could safely enjoy the "show," only to be moved to seats away from the windows so a couple of LAPD officers could occupy the booth for its vantage point. On her way home, she got pulled over on Foothill (she drove kind of a racy-looking Plymouth Barracuda). When the officer told her that it wasn't a good time to be out and asked her where she was going, she recalled saying—still perturbed about being moved from her window seat at Love's—"I'm cruising, of course!"

Anyway, it was fun times. The police had little choice but to aggressively put a lid on it. Things could not have continued the way they were going. So we went back to cruising on Van Nuys Boulevard on Wednesday nights.

On June 12, 1975, the *Crescenta Valley Ledger* printed an interesting story written by one of the "participants" in the Foothill Riots. The anonymous writer was actually the father of a teenager. He was forty-four years old, a college professor and a self-described "law-abiding citizen, a champion of our legal system, and a supporter of our police." He had read in the paper about the trouble on June 2, and knowing how teens are attracted to excitement, he knew that his son would want to go to the next Foothill Cruise Night on the eighth. He decided to adopt a proactive stance and take his son there himself. How much trouble could his son get in with his middle-aged dad in tow?

At about 9:30 p.m., they headed down to Foothill, parked on a side street just above and walked from there to the boulevard to watch the cruisers. From the writer's description, it sounds like he was near Lowell, ground zero of the worst of that particular night. They reached Foothill at 10:00 p.m., just in time to hear the police loudspeakers order the crowd to disperse. Father and son immediately turned back to head to the car, but the police line was sweeping down Foothill, and they were now cut off from the side street where their car was parked. Dad assumed that as an adult, and not the target of the sweep, they would let him go to his car and leave. He approached the police line and asked if he could pass through to get to his car. The officer barked at him, "Get your butt home fast or I'll take you in." Dad foolishly got a little indignant and replied, "It's not necessary to talk that way. We aren't doing anything wrong."

Dad and son were immediately handcuffed and zip-tied into a line of about one hundred other arrestees. They were quickly herded onto waiting buses for the trip to downtown Los Angeles. The dad related that he couldn't believe this was happening to him, that it had an unreal nightmare quality to it. At the county jail, they were fingerprinted, photographed, jailed, stripped, fingerprinted and photographed again and put into a large cell with the other arrestees. Once there, the father got a chance to talk to some of his fellow prisoners, who ranged in age from eighteen to well over fifty and from barefooted and longhaired to well dressed and conservative. Besides the cruise night kids caught in the sweep, the arrestees included a Foothill business owner who had stationed himself in front of his store to guard it, another business owner who was working late with his son and had made the mistake of stepping outside to watch the excitement and a shopper who had just emerged from a store with a bag of groceries.

Dad and son were bailed out the next morning and at the time of writing were awaiting arraignment for "failure to disperse." It was the first trouble with the law for both of them. Dad had a reflective attitude on the whole mess. He wrote that at first, he was furious and planned to sue the LAPD. Being arrested had been a degrading and physically painful experience. But after he cooled down, he came to the realization that he had put himself and his son in harm's way. Given the buildup to the June 8 event by the police, it was likely there would be trouble. Further, he realized he should not have tried to pass through the police line but instead should have gone the opposite way and circled back to his car. The police were on edge and nervous, maybe even fearful. He concluded he should have stayed away from them. It was bad judgment on his part. In an upbeat wrap-up to his story, he stated, "It brought my son and I closer together, and at what more appropriate time than just before Father's Day? I'm proud of my son, juvenile record and all, for he conducted himself like a man."

The next Monday cruise night on June 15 was met with a similar army of police, but the kids had gotten the message, and there were fewer participants. Foothill cruisers driving cars were harassed off the street, and for the most part, kids stood around on the sidewalk as the diminishing crowds were whittled down by police with arrests and citations. Only forty-nine were arrested that night.

The local *Ledger* newspaper summed up the event humorously: "Youngsters of the general area have been treated to a special night class in law enforcement, citizenship, drama and law. For the most part, they passed their final. Others were assigned field trips to the County Jail, and a series of lectures on government."

Although the teens thought having a Foothill Cruise Night would be fun, the rest of the community did not. People had moved to Crescenta Valley because of its quiet atmosphere, and they didn't want Foothill to become another Van Nuys Boulevard. The one and only official cruise night in the Crescenta Valley had started with a bang and ended with a whimper in only a month's time. Today, a few of those same Foothill cruisers, now grey, cruise to the weekly Saturday morning car show held at the UA Theater in La Cañada by the Early Rodders car club. Perhaps a couple of them are still driving the same muscle cars in which they briefly cruised on Foothill in 1975.

JOHN LEONARD ORR: FIREMAN AND ARSONIST

John Leonard Orr became a fireman and rose through the ranks to become captain and head arson investigator of Glendale Fire Department. In fact, he was able to investigate the very same fires that he was setting. Orr started his working career as a Sear's security guard and a clerk at a 7-11. He had originally wanted to become a police officer but failed his entrance exams. Instead, he became a dedicated fire investigator. Throughout the 1980s and 1990s, Los Angeles was plagued by a series of fires costing millions in damages and killing four people. Orr would later be found to be the instigator of most of these fires and was dubbed the "Pillow Pyro." His modus operandi was to set fires using a timed incendiary device. Fires were set in stores that were open for business and heavily populated. He also set small fires in the surrounding areas as diversions. On October 10, 1984, a major fire broke out in a hardware store on Orange Grove Avenue in South Pasadena. The store was completely destroyed, and four people died in the fire, including a grandmother and her two-year-old grandchild. Investigators declared it an electrical fire. Orr, however, insisted that it was arson. The victims were Jimmy Cetina (seventeen), Carolyn Kraus (twenty-six), Ada Deal (fifty) and her grandson Matthew Troidal (two). In January 1987, a convention of arson investigators took place in Fresno. During and after the convention, several

In 1987, the Montrose Theater burned down during the middle of the night under mysterious circumstances. Glendale Fire Department fire investigator John Orr, later convicted of numerous counts of arson, was one of the first on the scene. Although it was never proven, many locals still suspect that Orr was the source of the fire. *Pat Grant.*

suspicious fires were set in the area. Captain Marvin G. Casey of the Bakersfield Fire Department came to believe that an arson investigator from Los Angeles was responsible. He had recovered a fingerprint from a fire site but was unable to match it to anyone. In March 1989, another series of fires was set along the California coast in connection with a firefighter's conference in Pacific Grove. Captain Casey compiled a list of attendees at both conferences and came up with a short list of ten names. John Orr was on both lists. All ten on the short list were cleared at this time. In 1990–91, further investigation revealed that the previously unidentified fingerprint belonged to Orr. Orr was under investigation for several months in 1991. He was observed at the scene of a suspicious fire in November 1991 and finally arrested that December. Orr was tried for arson in August 1992, convicted and sentenced to three consecutive ten-year terms. One of the fires for which he was convicted destroyed sixty-seven homes in the College Hills section of Glendale. In June 1998, Orr was convicted of four counts of first-degree murder for the hardware store fire of 1984. The jury deadlocked on the death penalty, voting eight to four in favor of execution. Orr was sentenced to life plus twenty years.

Some arson investigators consider Orr to be one of the worst serial arsonists of the twentieth century. Investigators believe that he set nearly two thousand fires between 1984 and 1991. After his arrest, Foothill fires decreased by 90 percent. Orr continues to maintain his innocence, claiming that the legal system failed him. The full story of John Orr is recounted in Joseph Wambaugh's book *Fire Lover*. HBO made a movie dealing with the case called *Point of Origin*. Orr has written a fiction novel also called *Point of Origin*. The novel deals with a firefighter turned arsonist and closely follows Orr's real-life activities. In a twenty-one-year career, Orr rose to command an 8-man arson and explosives team and personally trained more than 1,200 firefighters and investigators. He videotaped many of his fires and always considered himself smarter than the police.

Chapter 8
Extreme Politics

The Battle of El Moreno Street

Historically, we here in the Crescenta Valley are no strangers to divisive politics of national impact. In fact, our little community hosted one of the initial battles of Cold War domestic politics in the form of a minor face-off between members of the Glendale American Legion and a local celebrity of leftist causes, Hugh Hardyman. That minor "battle" made national headlines. But more about that later. First, a little about the background of La Crescenta resident and political firebrand Hugh Hardyman.

To get a feel for who Hardyman was, we have to go all the way back to 1923, when our nation was embroiled in conflicts over labor versus capitalist conglomerates, punctuated by anarchist bomb plots. Upton Sinclair was a leader in liberal causes, having made his mark nationally with the publication of his novel *The Jungle* in 1906, which exposed the unsanitary and disgusting practices of the meatpacking industry. This led directly to the creation of the U.S. Food and Drug Administration.

In 1923, Sinclair took on the cause of a dockworkers' strike in San Pedro that had been broken by the LAPD and members of the Ku Klux Klan. He asked permission to hold a public meeting about the strike from then-mayor George Cryer, who pounded his desk, ranted about foreigners ruining our country and vowed to arrest Sinclair if he spoke. (As an aside, Cryer's family were briefly pioneers in La Crescenta, and little George had been in the first class of La Crescenta Elementary School. His name can be found on the plaque in front of the old school bell in front of today's La Crescenta Elementary, located at La Crescenta and Prospect. Cryer's reign as mayor of Los Angeles was marred with significant allegations of corruption, and portrayals of him as a Tammany Hall–style political boss are rife in Los Angeles–themed literature, from Raymond Chandler novels to the recent feature film *The Changeling*. That's Crescenta Valley's contribution to Los Angeles political history!) In spite of Mayor Cryer's admonition, Sinclair attended a rally of the striking dockworkers. He mounted a platform before a small crowd on Liberty Hill near the docks in San Pedro. He began to read the Bill of Rights, and ironically, as he read the First Amendment, which guarantees the right to free speech, he was arrested by the LAPD. His brother-in-law next took the platform and began to read from the Declaration of Independence. He was also promptly arrested. Another supporter took his place and protested the injustice, for which he, too, was manacled. Next, La Crescenta's own Hugh Hardyman took the stage and innocently remarked, "This is a most delightful climate," knowing that even a public comment on the weather would result in his immediate arrest, which it did.

The four were held incommunicado for eighteen hours on "suspicion of criminal syndicism" (whatever that means) until public pressure allowed for a lawyer to arrange bail. They were never charged. As a result of this incident, the American Civil Liberties Union (ACLU) of Southern California was formed, and it is still a dynamic political force today. A large plaque commemorating this significant event in Los Angeles history currently marks the site of Liberty Hill in San Pedro.

Upton Sinclair lived in Pasadena, close to Hardyman's Crescenta Valley home, so it was only natural that they continued their friendship. Hardyman led a small cadre of left-leaning politicos right here in the then very conservative Crescenta Valley. He was a leader of the Crescenta-Canada Democratic Club and was active with the Progressive Citizens of America, a meteoric political movement that advocated immediately after World War II for negotiations with the Soviet Union to slow down the quickly accelerating Cold War. His views came into direct conflict with the conservative views of the community. Hardyman hosted political meetings at his home in the 2300 block of El Moreno Street, a quiet street of beautiful homes, just off Briggs above Foothill. These meetings featured several notable speakers, including Nobel Prize–winning professor Linus Pauling, who advocated demilitarization of our relations in Europe. It was these meetings that raised the ire of local conservatives and set the stage for an inevitable showdown, known nationally as the "Battle of La Crescenta" and locally as the "Battle of El Moreno Street."

On November 14, 1947, a regular meeting of the Crescenta-Canada Democratic Club was in progress at the Hardyman home. Thirty-some local Democrats sat in Hardyman's living room discussing club business. Their guest that evening, David Leff, a former information officer for the United Nations Relief and Rehabilitation Administration, had just returned from a food distribution mission to postwar Yugoslavia and was there to discuss aspects of the Marshall Plan.

Suddenly, twenty men, most of them wearing American Legion caps, entered the front door and quickly made their way through the home, covering every window and door. The air was tense as Hardyman calmly invited his new uninvited guests to find a seat. Leff, visibly nervous, asked if the American Legion often took over meetings here. Two reporters were on the scene, and cameras started flashing immediately. One had come with the invaders, while the other, a *Crescenta Valley Ledger* reporter, happened to be on scene covering the Democrat meeting. His photos are the most interesting, featuring uneasy glares from the invaders and their hands trying to block the lens of the camera.

Hardyman stated that he was shoved from the front of the assembled group as a leader of the invaders began to read from a prepared statement. The leader addressed the group as being members of the Progressive Citizens of America, to which Hardyman objected, stating that although he was a PCA member, this was a meeting of the Democratic Club. The leader of the invaders refuted that and continued to address the crowd as the PCA, proceeding with his edict. He identified his own group as veterans of World War I and World War II and members of the Americanization Committee for Community Betterment. He first told the assembled Democrats that this was not a raid and that no one would be hurt. He told the group their activities had been monitored because the PCA was attempting to destroy our form of government. He then warned the group that the PCA would not be tolerated in this area: "We will give you just 10 minutes to forget this meeting and go back to your own homes and thank God that you live in the United States. And we will not warn you again!" There was next a shouted order to "Proceed according to the plan!" after which the invaders left the house. A few of the Democrats, not bargaining for this kind of

American Legion members guard the exits of Hugh Hardyman's home. The Legion members look a little dubious in this shot, perhaps not expecting the press to be present with cameras. *Katherine Halford.*

conflict, followed the edict and left. The sheriff was immediately called, and two patrol cars soon arrived. By then, the invaders were gone. No arrests were made, and the meeting continued. Leff regained his composure and continued with the program, speaking to the remaining group about the political aspects of relief efforts in Yugoslavia.

In retrospect, it's fairly obvious that this event was somewhat of a comedy of errors. The Legionnaires certainly thought they were doing their patriotic duty in breaking up a meeting of the PCA. However, they were clearly way off the mark. They were just beginning a national pastime of looking for "a Red under every bed" that would consume much of the '50s.

Hardyman, however, always ready to take up a cause, would have none of the idea that this was a mistake. The real battle was now on with the full weight of his fervor—the bloodless "Battle of El Moreno" was about to get bloody!

The next morning, Hardyman, with news reporters in tow, was down at the Montrose Sheriff's Station to press charges, alleging that the intruders had been armed and had "roughed up" his guests. His next stop was the district attorney's office in Los Angeles, where, according to the *Ledger*, the incident began to flicker onto the national news. As the heat began to rise, the raiding party sheepishly turned themselves in, and the participants were revealed to have indeed been members of Glendale's American Legion Post 127, including the post commander. They were all charged with breaking up a lawful meeting and disturbing the peace, save for one participant, a former publisher of the *Glendale News Press*, who was charged with battery.

Hardyman continued to spin the incident. A week later, he organized a mass meeting featuring nationally prominent political figures at the Glendale Civic Auditorium to condemn the act. The incident was even discussed on the floor of Congress. However, when the trial concluded a month later, only thirteen of the twenty charged were convicted. Eleven received $25 fines or a 5-day suspended sentence, and two, including the *News Press* publisher, received a $250 fine or 125 days. Hardyman felt this was too lenient, and the lawsuits began to fly.

According to the *Los Angeles Times*, the first stop was the U.S. District Court, where allegations of civil rights violations were dismissed. Next up was the U.S. Circuit Court, where that dismissal was reversed. The third level of the judicial system to hear Hardyman's case was the Superior Court, which found in favor of the Legionnaires. Finally, in 1951, Hardyman pushed his case all the way to the U.S. Supreme Court. The Supreme Court denied Hardyman's claims of civil rights violation in a 6–3 decision, stating that the Civil Rights Act did not cover such privately instituted damage suits. Justice Jackson spoke for the majority, calling the incident "a lawless political brawl, precipitated by a handful of white citizens against other white citizens." He added, "The facts alleged fall far short of a conspiracy to…deny equality of rights under the law."

And so the "Battle of El Moreno Street" ended with a whimper, but Hardyman's penchant for making headlines was still on a hot streak. This is where our story is picked up by Pasadena historian Matt Hormann, who recently wrote about Hardyman's eventual fate. In 1952, in the middle of the Korean War, La Crescenta's Hugh Hardyman, again per the *Times*, traveled to Red China to join the Chinese in condemning the United States for using germ warfare on North Korea. Confessions from captured U.S. pilots obtained by the Chinese confirmed that the pilots had participated in dropping plague and cholera-infected insects. Hardyman continued to tour other Communist countries, issuing the same condemnation. (Interestingly, that allegation that the United States employed germ warfare in Korea still rages across the Internet today.) When Hardyman returned to the States in 1955, he was collared by the infamous House Un-American Activities Committee (HUAC), a formidable group of members of the U.S. House of Representatives, whose goal was to ferret out communists from positions of influence. HUAC subpoenaed Hardyman, grilled him on his trip to Communist China and questioned his patriotism. Hardyman cited the Constitution as his defense and, for the most part, quipped witty answers to their questions. In the end, he chastised them for "their rather un-American doctrine of 'guilt by association.'" HUAC responded by stating, "While he denied actual Communist Party membership, Mr. Hardyman betrayed himself as a staunch supporter of the party by repeating his heinous propaganda statements at committee hearings."

At this point, Hardyman apparently left La Crescenta for a home in Topanga Canyon, where he helped organize the Ormsby Village for Youth, a camp for underprivileged kids sponsored by the First Unitarian Church of Los Angeles. After helping to establish similar camps in Vermont and Northern Mexico, Hardyman died in 1960. His name lives on at the at the First Unitarian Church in Los Angeles, where the Hugh Hardyman Center was established by his friend Linus Pauling, who used the proceeds from his two Nobel Peace Prizes to fund construction. In La Crescenta, in a quiet, tree-shaded house in the 2300 block of El Moreno Street, current residents are probably unaware that their home once hosted one of the minor battles of the Cold War, the "Battle of El Moreno Street."

THE CONSERVATIVE HEART OF A CONSERVATIVE HEARTLAND

In the late 1960s and early 1970s, the John Birch Society, a patriotic anti-Communist organization, was headquartered in San Marino. Congressman John Russolot was a member. It was estimated that the society was quite active in La Cañada. Two chapters are reportedly active today. Up until the 1990s, the foothill communities were solidly Republican and conservative. Frank Lanterman represented the area in the assembly for twenty-eight years. Other conservative leaders included John Harmer, Ed Reinecke, Carlos Moorhead, Newt Russell and our current Los Angeles County supervisor, Mike Antonovich. In 1964, La Cañada voted 3.5–1.0 for Barry Goldwater. Democrats were a rarity. Today, due to changing demographics, the area tends to vote more Democratic.

Anti-Radicalism in the Foothills

The ACLU of Southern California was founded in reaction to the arrest and jailing of Upton Sinclair in 1923. Sinclair was arrested for reading the First Amendment in San Pedro. He was speaking on behalf of the striking dockworkers. Hugh Hardyman of La Crescenta was arrested for giving a weather report. They were arrested for violating the criminal syndical laws. The Sheriff, in making the arrests, said that he had "heard enough about Constitutional Rights." In 1935, Chapter 41 of the Disabled American Veterans sponsored an Americanization program in the Foothills. The group was cooperating with all organizations in fighting the enemies of the U.S. government. In 1950, the *Crescenta Valley Ledger* newspaper warned La Crescenta residents to be aware and prepared to meet the Communist challenge. The paper quoted the FBI as having a list of six thousand known communists residing in California, a number second only to New York. This was a huge percentage of Communists, as the known national membership of the party was only twenty-five thousand. The *Ledger* editorial warned that this area was especially vulnerable to sabotage and that Communists were prepared to bring families to their knees. The *Ledger* encouraged the community to come to a meeting at the sheriff's station in Montrose to consider what was ahead and how to effectively combat it. Trained observers and experts on Communist procedure would outline what lie ahead. The *Ledger* encouraged the community to not wait for a directive from our monumentally fumbling government bureaucracy. It stated that the valley had the vision, patriotism, leadership and loyalty to combat the rising Red Tide. The local chapter of the Valley Americanism Educational League held its second organizational meeting on August 25, 1950, at the American

In the 1950s and '60s, the *Crescenta Valley Ledger* was the voice of ultra-conservative politics under the leadership of Don Carpenter. Promotion of the John Birch Society, anti-Communism, urging America's withdrawal from the United Nations and support of the Vietnam War were some of the *Ledger*'s pet editorial subjects. This was the paper's office just east of Montrose. *Glendale Public Library.*

Legion Memorial Hall. The league claimed twenty-five years of experience in battling Communism and was at that time sponsoring a petition to outlaw the Communist movement. It favored the internment of Communists and the seizure of their records and propaganda. One had to sign a loyalty oath to join the league. Clarence Christenson was the temporary chairman, and Bob Andlson of Los Angeles City College was to be the speaker. How American could the league be when it proposed the violation of the First, Fourth and Fifth Amendments to the Constitution?

In 1955, Ed Gibbons, Communist foe, spoke at the Veterans of Foreign Wars, Crescenta Valley post. Ed Gibbons was a noted anti-Communist who had appeared in many debates and television programs. He was a fiery champion of the constitution. A film was to be shown that outlined the methods by which communists exerted their influence to confuse and distort American governmental procedures. In January 1955, the *Ledger* published a call to arms. The subject was a rally in Los Angeles to show how Communism was using the churches. It was to be the second "Faith and

Cold War paranoia of the 1950s fostered a military feel in the Crescenta Valley. In this nighttime civil defense drill held on the playground of La Crescenta Elementary School, police muster next to local volunteer block captains of the Federal Civil Defense Administration. They were training to deal with the aftermath of a nuclear attack. *Historical Society of the Crescenta Valley.*

A Chrysler V-8-powered air raid siren overlooks the Crescenta Valley soon after its installation in 1955. The rotating siren produced a 138-decibal wail that carried for miles. Its signal was designed to send Crescenta Valley residents into their backyard bomb shelters or to duck-and-cover in an interior hallway. This rusting remnant of the Cold War still stands atop Cerro Negro in the San Rafael Mountains above La Cañada. *Glendale Public Library.*

Freedom" rally at the Shrine Auditorium. The featured speaker was Dr. Carl McIntire, president of the International Council of Christian Churches. His subject would be "Christian Repudiation of Co-Existence." All of these efforts must have paid off because Communism did not win, and we are still free Americans.

Nazis Return

In 1964, George Lincoln Rockwell designated Glendale as the West Coast headquarters of the American Nazi Party (ANP). The headquarters was located in the 800 block of East Colorado and remained open until the early 1980s. Rockwell was a veteran of World War II. After the war, however, he came to the conclusion that the wrong side had won. The ANP wanted to create a pure white race. It denied the truth of the Holocaust and professed its allegiance only to selected parts of the U.S. Constitution. It claimed to not hate other racial groups but did believe in strict racial segregation. Its headquarters in Glendale was called the "White House."

Glendale was a very different community in 1964, composed of predominantly white and northern European residents. Rockwell chose Glendale because it was, as he stated, "a white man's town." If Rockwell believed the city would welcome him, he was in for a big surprise. On December 4, 1964, hundreds of angry phone calls poured into city offices. The calls demanded that the city ban the Nazi Party from Glendale. Thus began a protracted fight to drive out the Nazis. Ralph Forbes, Rockwell's local lieutenant, set up his headquarters as a residence and meeting place. The landlord was unaware of what he had done. The city contended that the house could not be used for dual purposes and refused to turn on the home's electricity. The Nazis met by candlelight. The city then took the matter to the courts. It maintained that the Nazis needed a permit to have large numbers of people in a single-family home. On December 28, 1964, Forbes and four others were arraigned on charges of violating the building code. They were charged with operating a meeting hall in a residential home without a special permit, fined $300 and sentenced to six months in jail. On April 29, 1965, Forbes was convicted of zoning violations. The decision was overturned on appeal. Author Gary Keyes relates his own encounter with the Glendale Nazis: "My experience with

Above: In December 1964, this rented house on Colorado Boulevard in Glendale was the national headquarters of the American Nazi Party, Western Division. It became the focus of many protests. *www.pojawa.com.*

Left: Ralph Forbes was the Western Division commander of the American Nazi Party. This photo from Christmas 1964 shows him in uniform looking at Christmas cards in front of his fireplace in Glendale. Above the mantel is a portrait of Hitler atop crossed American flags. *AP photo/ David F. Smith.*

Glendale Nazis took place in December 1964. I was a student at UCSB researching right-wing extremism. I stood outside the headquarters trying to build up enough courage to walk into the building. Being young and unsure of myself, I couldn't do it. I saw a person in the back of the house and thought I could talk to him one on one. The person I talked to was not an official Nazi, but his racist views had earned him honorary membership." On August 12, 1965, three Nazis were put on trial for disturbing the peace and endangering public health. At the same time, counter demonstrations were taking place at the Thrifty Mart Plaza in North Glendale, which had been accused of racial discrimination. On January 10, 1966, the Glendale Kiwanis pledged to use all resources to get the ANP out of town. On August 25, 1967, George Lincoln Rockwell was murdered by a former party member. Shortly before his death, Rockwell had changed the name of the party to the National Socialist White People's Party. The party then relocated its main headquarters to El Monte.

In the 1980s, Nazi propaganda reappeared in our area. In June 1987, six teens were arrested on suspicion of terrorism and conspiracy. They were in possession of white supremacist fliers and stickers that had been posted on storefronts and utility poles in Montrose.

THE PACE AMENDMENT

The Pace Amendment was to spark controversy and a race riot in Glendale in the 1980s. William Daniel Johnson is a Brigham Young University graduate who majored in Japanese and served a mission in Japan. He earned his law degree from Columbia University in 1981. A resident of Glendale and La Cañada, he wrote the Pace Amendment under the assumed identity of "James O. Pace"—one of three identities he has used. The Pace Amendment would repeal the Fourteenth and Fifteenth amendments of the U.S. Constitution and use welfare money to deport all people ineligible for U.S. citizenship. The amendment reads, "No person shall be a citizen of the U.S. unless he is a non-Hispanic white of the European race...Only citizens shall have the right and privilege to reside permanently in the United States." According to the amendment, Native Americans and Hawaiians would be maintained on reservations. Johnson hoped to "avert the decline and fall of

America." According to him, racial mixing and diversity was causing social and cultural disintegration. In 1986, he proposed his amendment to the Neo-Nazi World Congress of Aryan Nations. On June 26, 1987, a debate was scheduled between Johnson and the Glendale Human Relations council at the Glendale Public Library. Neo-Nazis, KKK and the Jewish Defense League clashed in front of the library. The brawl was noisy and bloody. The fight was stopped by the Glendale Police. In August 1989, a bomb went off in Johnson's Glendale headquarters. John Orr of the Glendale Fire Department's Arson and Explosives squad estimated that $5,000 damage was done. Johnson moved to Casper, Wyoming, where, in 1989, he ran for Dick Cheney's vacant congressional seat. His campaign manager was a member of the KKK. He returned to Glendale in 1990 to run for Superior Court judge. He did not win either of those two elections. In 2006, he ran in the Democratic primary for Congress. He was defeated. In September 2007, he hosted a $2,000-a-plate fundraiser for Ron Paul in Glendale. In October 2010, he helped found the American Freedom Party to represent the political interests of white Americans. He continues to espouse his racist views in the area today.

The Good, the Bad and the Ugly

The Foothills have given to California three lieutenant governors: Robert H. Finch, Ed Reinecke and John Harmer.

Robert Finch

Robert Finch, after graduating from Occidental College in 1947, went on to a long and distinguished political career. He began as an administrative aid to Los Angeles mayor Norris Poulson. He then helped Richard Nixon win reelection to Congress in 1948. In 1951, Nixon advised Finch to earn a law degree from USC. Finch served in the U.S. Marine Corps from 1951 to 1953 during the Korean War. He practiced law between 1953 and 1958. In 1958, he became the administrative assistant to Vice President Richard Nixon, and in 1960, he managed Nixon's presidential campaign. In 1966, he won the post of lieutenant governor of California, gaining more votes than governor-elect Ronald Reagan. His future was bright, and he seemed well on his way to the U.S. Senate. In 1968, Nixon asked Finch to be his vice president. Finch declined the honor. If he had accepted, he would have become president in 1973 when Nixon resigned. Finch was the closest friend that Nixon ever had. Nixon attended Finch's daughter's wedding at the Church of the Lighted Window in La Cañada. Nixon's Secret Service detail was thrown into chaos on that day. The Secret Service had all of the security for the president set up on one side of the car. Nixon surprised them by exiting on the opposite side. What the Secret Service did not know was that due to La Cañada's conservative nature, if a Republican president was not safe in La Cañada, he was not safe anywhere. When Nixon became president, he asked Finch to be his secretary of Health, Education and Welfare (HEW). Finch didn't want the job (he was planning on running for the U.S. Senate), but out of loyalty to Nixon, he reluctantly accepted.

Finch strongly enforced the Supreme Court's decision on school integration and the Civil Rights Act of 1964–65. This, however, ran afoul of Nixon's "Southern Strategy," so Finch was removed as secretary of HEW. HEW strongly opposed the removal of Finch and protested by going on a three-day strike. Finch was eventually made a counselor to the president but found himself frozen out of the inner circle. This turned out to be his good fortune. He resigned in December 1972 and returned to California. He had no personal involvement in Watergate, but his association with Nixon ruined his political future. He was defeated in the Republican Senate primary in 1976 by S.I. Hiyakawa. He died at the age of ninety in Pasadena.

Ed Reinecke

Governor Ronald Reagan picked Ed Reinecke to replace Robert Finch as lieutenant governor on January 21, 1969. He was reelected on November 9, 1970, but resigned on November 2, 1974. Reinecke was born in Medford, Oregon. He graduated from Beverly Hills High School in 1942. During World War II, he served in the U.S. Navy. He then attended Caltech and earned a degree in mechanical engineering. He entered politics in 1965, at which time he was elected to the House of Representatives. He served in the House until 1969, when he became lieutenant governor. In 1984, he appeared to be on his way to becoming governor—he was popular, photogenic and flush with campaign money. However, after he was indicted on three counts of perjury in the Watergate scandal, campaign money suddenly disappeared, and he lost the Republican primary to Pete Wilson. Reinecke was convicted of perjury and was given a suspended sentence of eighteen months. He resigned as lieutenant governor one day before his sentencing. His conviction for perjury was overturned on a technicality. Ten years after his conviction, Reinecke was back in the saddle as the chairman of the California Republican Party. In 1983, he was fifty-nine and considered himself too old to be governor. He should point the age factor out to our current (2014) governor, Jerry Brown.

John Harmer

Harmer served in the California State Senate from 1966 to 1974. He was appointed lieutenant governor in 1974 and served until 1975. He was the second man appointed to that position by Governor Ronald Reagan. Harmer has also served as chairman of the Lighted Candle Society. This organization is opposed to pornography and has filed briefs with the U.S. Supreme Court. Harmer has written a book titled *A War We Must Win*, which details his forty-year war on pornography. As a California senator, Harmer was a vigilant foe of pornography. His crusade against pornography provoked one of the local newspapers to ask in an editorial, "Just what is Senator Harmer's fascination with pornography?" Today, Harmer resides in Bountiful, Utah.

Barry Goldwater Jr.

Barry Goldwater Jr. served in the House of Representatives from 1969 to 1982. He represented the Foothill Communities. Barry graduated from the Stauton Military Academy in 1957 and Arizona State University in 1962. He worked as a stockbroker and as a public relations executive before being elected to Congress. As a congressman, Barry was considered to be "cool." He tooled around the congressional building on a skateboard and allegedly smoked pot in his office. In 1982, he ran for the U.S. Senate against Pete Wilson. Goldwater lost and claimed that it was due to partisan mudslinging. His name had been linked to a congressional drug-use scandal. Goldwater was found not to be involved in the drug scandal; however, he did seek help from a Wickenburg, Arizona treatment center for a drinking and cocaine problem. He was able to successfully overcome these problems.

Goldwater's first marriage broke up in the mid-'70s after a woman he was dating, Loretta Clark Guinan, disappeared. Guinan was married to Michael Guinan, an accused thief. Loretta had agreed to testify against her husband, and Michael was suspected in his wife's disappearance. In November 2008, Goldwater ran for vice president with Ron Paul on the Louisiana ballot. They ran on the platform of the Louisiana Taxpayers Party. Goldwater received 9,368 votes for vice president, enough to place him third in the popular vote. Today, he lives in Phoenix, Arizona, near his son Barry Goldwater III.

PAT NOLAN: FROM TOMMY TROJAN TO FEDERAL PRISONER 06833-097

Patrick Nolan attended USC and rode the school's mascot, Traveler, at the football games. In 1978, the twenty-eight-year-old was elected to the California State Assembly, where he represented Glendale, Burbank, Toluca Lake and Sunland-Tujunga. He was reelected and served until 1984, when he was elected assembly leader, a position he held until 1988. His future seemed unlimited. Nolan's political philosophy was so conservative that he picketed the KKK for espousing socialism. While at USC, he helped to hang Jane Fonda in effigy. He criticized Senator George Deukmejian as being too liberal. His political beliefs marked him as one of the "cavemen" in the state legislature. Nolan had aspirations of becoming assembly speaker and running for statewide office and perhaps even governor. His hopes were dashed by a series of setbacks that led to his resignation from the leadership position. Nolan's power was weakened by his role in a 1986 scheme to forge President Reagan's signature on the campaign letters of GOP Assembly candidates. A Sacramento district attorney report released in September 1989 alleged that Nolan had asked his staff to lie to White House officials who were looking into the incident. Nolan was one of four legislators targeted in an FBI sting in which federal agents created phony companies, sponsored bills and paid money to lawmakers while seeking legislative favors in return. Indicted for money laundering, extortion, conspiracy and racketeering, Nolan pleaded guilty to one count of racketeering in 1984. He was convicted along with

Senator Joseph B. Montoya and Assemblyman Frank Hill. One week after pleading guilty, he was professing his innocence and showing no contrition: "They won't shut me up!" Nolan served two years in a federal prison and several months in a halfway house. Prison softened his hard line on criminals. The former advocate of the death penalty stated in 1998 that drug abusers and nonviolent prisoners might be spending too much time in jail. He has recently become an advocate of prison reform.

Chapter 9
Mean Mother Nature

Earth, Wind, Fire and Flood: Natural Disasters

People who have immigrated to California to escape the rigors of the extreme weather in other parts of the country seem to forget why they moved to California in the first place. They are always complaining that California has no seasons. Those of us who have enjoyed California know this is not true. California does have seasons—they are well known to us as earthquake season, wind season, fire season and flood season! Small twisters and waterspouts seem to be a recent addition to our climate. There have been too many natural disasters in the Foothill communities to be covered in a work of this length. Flood following fire is a recurring story in the Foothills. The residents in the Foothills, being of pioneering stock, take each disaster in stride. We take pride in surviving the worst that nature can dish out. It is the price we pay for living in one of the best places in the world.

Earthquakes are a fact of life in California. One geologist has said, "If you saw a fault line map of Los Angeles, it would look like six panes of glass that had been dropped from five feet. The fault lines are everywhere." Californians accept that earthquakes are a fact of life, just as easterners accept their hurricanes and tornadoes. Earthquakes that tend to terrify Los Angeles newcomers are ignored by longtime residents. The Foothills suffered serious damage due to a tornado and hurricane-force winds in 1964. The twister destroyed the home of Dr. William S. Leonard of Tujunga. The house of Donald Rowe, his next-door neighbor, was also damaged, as were six other homes in the path of the twister. Throughout the Greater Los Angeles area, more than ten thousand homes and businesses were damaged by winds in excess of one hundred miles per hour. In Montrose and Verdugo City, plate glass windows and electric signs were damaged. Automobile dealership Fred Hauter Ford lost three windows and a roof. Among the other stores that were damaged were Kimmel-Meehan, Penny's, Montrose Shopping Bag and Sport Chalet. Many trees and walls were destroyed throughout the city. The wind damage was estimated at $2 million, but this was insignificant when compared to the $5 million in damage caused by the fire that was aided by that same wind. Because of the wind, the Foothills found itself fighting two fires at the same time. Fires struck the San Rafael Mountains and the Verdugo Mountains, which were declared disaster areas by city, county and state officials. The fire consumed 9,100 acres. It began at 5:47 a.m. in Whiting Woods and jumped from canyon to canyon, burning over the Verdugos toward Burbank and down to Kenneth Road in Glendale. Residents of Glendale, Burbank, Pasadena, Eagle Rock and the Foothills were forced to evacuate their homes. Four homes in Glendale were engulfed, and seven homes in Eagle Rock burned. Local high school and college students aided firefighters in their efforts to control the blaze. The Foothills have suffered major fires in 1906, 1909, 1927, 1964, 1965, 1970, 1975 and 2008, which saw the worst fire, known locally as the "Station Fire."

A small fire of three hundred acres hit La Crescenta on May 17, 1906. A firebreak was built under the supervision of forest ranger Philip Begue. The firebreak ran along the base of Dunsmore Canyon to Gould Castle on the edge of Pickens Canyon. The firebreak was considered a precaution to protect the forest reserve from any fires that might start in the lower valley.

Fires swept the Foothills on September 12, 1908. Rangers and volunteers were pressed into service to keep the brush fire from overwhelming the local communities. The fire in the Sierra Madre Foothills burned orchards, farms and homes. The fire began on the ranch of Reverend S.L. Ward of Glendale, who was burning brush on his ten-acre tract in La Crescenta. He had a permit and had taken all the proper precautions. When he began, the wind was calm, but it later rose and spread the fire beyond his control. The fire spread from La Crescenta into Tujunga Valley. Lines of rangers and citizens drafted from neighboring villages fought the fire on the mountain

Windstorms have been a major theme in the destructive natural forces in the valley. This "Santa Ana" windstorm took place in 1964 and wreaked havoc on this home with gusts up to one hundred miles per hour. *Glendale Public Library*.

Wildfire is an ever-present danger in the Crescenta Valley. In this photo taken from Honolulu Avenue in Montrose in the 1960s, the Verdugo Mountains blaze away, threatening homes on the edges of the valley. *Glendale Public Library*.

ridge, as it could not be stopped before that point. As the fire raged, the volunteers became exhausted, and many left for home. The fire crew was reduced to only fifty men and rangers. Forest supervisor Charlton took his entire office staff to fight the fire. The fire was plainly visible from Pasadena and Los Angeles. You have probably noticed from this account that the Foothills had no official fire protection at this time. The communities had to rely on volunteer efforts until 1920.

In 1920, A.A. Lester was appointed deputy fire warden. His equipment consisted of a fire trailer and equipment financed by the community. A fire protection district was formed in Flintridge in 1924, and in 1925, John Gates was appointed captain of a one-man unit. He was stationed on Inverness in Flintridge. In December 1924, another station was established on Hermosa Avenue in Montrose under the command of A.R. Duncan. On August 12, 1929, a stone fire station was built next to St. Luke's Church on Foothill Boulevard at a cost of $7,614. The stone building is still in existence today. The station's crew consisted of four regulars and two volunteers under the command of Captain Floyd J. Lee.

The fire of 1933 was responsible for the disastrous flood of 1934. The fire destroyed the ground cover, and when the clouds burst on New Year's Eve, there was nothing to hold back the floodwaters. This disaster is well covered by Art Cobery in his book *The Great Crescenta Valley Flood*. Combating the fire were six hundred men and two thousand boys from local CCC camps. They battled the fire for ninety-two hours in three shifts, sleeping only ten hours during the battle. They made their stand at Briggs Terrace, Pennsylvania Avenue and Orange Street. The fire destroyed at least ten homes and cabins. There was little hope in controlling the blaze. The consensus was that the fire would have to burn itself out. The fire had begun in Pickens Canyon and swept west to Dunsmore Canyon. It would burn within fifty feet of Foothill Boulevard. The fire burned out Pickens Canyon completely and burned six homes on Briggs Terrace. It also destroyed one home on New York Avenue and three in Tujunga. The fire burned for three days and destroyed one building at the Ananda Ashrama. Patients at the Hillcrest Sanitarium were evacuated to hospitals in Glendale. The Hermitage Mountain Vineyard (now Deukmejian Park) was partially destroyed.

In addition to the fear of forest fires in October and November 1965, the Foothills experienced ten arson fires set by professional firebugs in La Crescenta and Glendale. Damage was estimated at $130,000. All buildings were unoccupied at the start of the fires. Norman Stolley of the Glendale Fire Department said that the nature of the fires indicated that they had been set by professionals. Fires were set in the 3600 block of Los Amigos in La Crescenta and the 3700 block of North Verdugo at Swanson's Furniture. Fires also struck the 3300 block of Sparr Boulevard. A home and store in Montrose were burned. In addition, two fires were set at Anawalt Lumber in Montrose and the Church of Religious Science on Santa Carlotta. The church sustained several thousand dollars worth of damage, and the social hall was completely gutted. The parish house of St. George's Episcopal Church suffered extensive damage as well. It was the second fire at the parish house within three weeks. Also included in the damages of the fires was a church in La Crescenta, a home on Hermosita in the Verdugo Woodlands and the La Crescenta Women's Club.

Floods have also impacted the area. The New Year's Eve flood of 1934 was the worst, but floods also hit the area in 1938, 1978 and 2009. The Pinecrest flood of 1978 followed a forest fire that torched the front range of the San Gabriel Mountains in 1975. The mountain vegetation had not sufficiently grown back in 1978 when the rains came. On the morning of the flood, Vern Deuck, a Crescenta Valley High School teacher, stepped out of his front door in time to see a wall of water, rock, dirt and cars go tearing down Pine Cone Road. The Genophiles' home was directly in the path. Thirty other homes were also destroyed. Fortunately, no one was injured, but many residents were trapped inside of their homes. The Genophiles' children, Scott and Kim, ran to their parents' room and jumped on the bed. The floodwaters took the mattress almost to the ceiling. The house was filled with mud, and the yard became a parking lot for thirteen cars that had been washed down the hill by the floodwaters. Charles Hull of 5400 Pine Cone Road saw his car and others wash down the hill. Mrs. June Bar, a teacher at Rosemont Intermediate School, also lost her car. On Ocean View Boulevard, Jay Ingleson's home at 2100 Earnslow was flooded. On Durwood, Bill and Robin Geers' home was flooded for the third time in eleven years. Damage was also reported on Dunsmore and Lowell and in Whiting Woods. The events of 1975–78 were to be repeated in 2009–10.

The Station Fire of August 25, 2008, is thought to have been caused by arson. The fired burned 160,000 acres and threatened the communities of La Cañada, Flintridge, Glendale, Acton, La Crescenta, Little Rock, Altadena and Sunland-Tujunga. It destroyed 209 structures, 89 of which were homes. Just as the Foothill Fire of 1933 denuded the mountains of their ground cover, the fire of 2008 caused a repeat. Between February 5 and 6, Los Angeles received over four inches of rain. On February 6, at 4:45 a.m., the debris basin on Manistee Road was clogged with a nine-ton boulder. This triggered severe debris and mudflows between Manistee and Ocean View Boulevard. The rocks, debris and cars that came cascading down Ocean View Boulevard and Rock Castle Drive sounded like thunder. At least 540 homes were evacuated. Thunderous mudslides damaged 40 homes, 30 of them on Ocean View Boulevard alone. Cars and furniture were swept down the hill, and some homes were filled up to the roofline with rocks and mud. Twenty-five cars were damaged or destroyed. Today, most of the K-Rails that were put in place for protection from further slides have been removed. There are a few still up, though, as a precaution and reminder of the dangers of Mother Nature.

The Struggle for Water

If you live in Los Angeles, you know that you live in a desert. The fight for water and water rights has been a constant battle from the earliest times in the Crescenta-Cañada Valley. In the late 1800s, armed men guarded their own water. Theodor Pickens was one of the first residents of the valley, settling here in 1871. Understanding the importance of water, he chose his home carefully so that he could control the water source. Pickens claimed the water rights of Pickens Canyon, the main water source for the valley. In 1874, Colonel Adolfus Williams and Dr. Jacob Lanterman purchased the Mexican land grant "Rancho La Cañada" for $10,000.00, or $1.60 an acre. The huge amount of land was able to be purchased at a ridiculously low price because at the time, it had little or no water. Pickens, who controlled all of the water at the time, refused to sell it to Williams and Lanterman at a reasonable price. The battle between the three men went on for two years. The story is that Amoretta Lanterman took matters into her own hands, grabbing a shotgun and riding up to deal with Pickens herself. The story may or may not be true, but it makes for a great image. Water rights were eventually secured for Lanterman and Williams, and the growth of the valley was assured.

Chapter 10
Sanitariums

Sanitariums in La Crescenta

Sanitariums were one of the main industries of our early Crescenta Valley. Today, we generally think of sanitariums as being lockup facilities for the insane, but that was not the case in the early days of sanitariums. They were facilities to care for any chronic diseases, physical or mental, and the Crescenta Valley had sanitariums of both kinds.

Dr. Benjamin Briggs, in addition to founding La Crescenta in 1881, also established the valley's reputation for treatment of illness, and the area became famous for its healthful climate and availability of treatment centers. Several lung disease hospitals were established here, including Utley's Sanitarium at the top of Briggs (just below Briggs's home); Mount Lukens Sanitarium, now the site of Dunsmore Park; and Hillcrest Sanitarium at the top of Lowell. Several small sanitariums, basically larger homes converted to accept patients, thrived here as well. By the late 1920s, there were a score or more treatment facilities here for ailments like tuberculosis, bronchitis and even asthma.

Along with the medical sanitariums, mental sanitariums began to pop up. Kimball Sanitarium, where Ralph's is today, treated insanity and drug addiction and has provided a treasure-trove of infamous stories for

Rockhaven Sanitarium operated as a high-class facility for women from 1923 until 2006. The City of Glendale purchased the historic property in 2008, and today it awaits its next phase of existence as a park and community center. The volunteer group Friends of Rockhaven maintain the still-furnished interiors and give tours of the three-and-a-half-acre site. *Photo by Mike Lawler.*

historians. Rockhaven Sanitarium was more sedate, having been created for women with mental and emotional issues, eventually specializing in elderly patients suffering from dementia. Rockhaven, located on Honolulu between La Crescenta and Rosemont, is the only sanitarium that has survived intact. But there are several bits and pieces of defunct sanitariums all around Crescenta Valley.

The origins of the sanitarium industry in Crescenta Valley are rooted firmly in the treatment of tuberculosis. In the nineteenth century, as urban areas in Europe and the eastern United States crowded people together, tuberculosis (TB) became rampant. TB was little understood, and it wasn't until the 1870s that it was recognized as being contagious. There was no treatment or cure, and contracting the disease was usually a death sentence.

It was at about this time that a successful fruit grower in Santa Paula, Benjamin Briggs, lost his wife to TB. Having lung problems of his own, possibly related to a gunshot wound to his lung he had suffered years before, or perhaps due to his own TB infection, he embarked on a quest to find a cure for the disease. Being well off financially, he traveled the world, educating himself on the latest theories on TB and radical new treatment methods. One theory gaining popularity at that time was that air quality could favorably affect the progression of the disease. Many TB sufferers were heading for drier climates in the western United States, hoping that clean, pure air, along with a dose of the physical rigors of an outdoor lifestyle, would save their lives. This fruit grower turned doctor latched on to this idea. He wanted to establish a hospital for the treatment of TB and other lung diseases, and he searched for the best location, eventually deciding on the foothills of the San Gabriel Mountains. In 1881, Dr. Briggs purchased what is now known as Briggs Terrace, located at the top of Briggs Avenue, to establish one of the early sanitariums of the western United States.

Whether Dr. Briggs was successful in treating any patients has never been recorded. Letters written by Dr. Briggs's second wife imply that although Briggs came to Crescenta Valley intending to start a sanitarium, he was too weak from his own TB to ever achieve his goal. No official records exist of him ever treating anyone, although one newspaper article from 1892 reports several people "convalescing" at his home, which would perhaps indicate some sort of treatment was occurring. We hear anecdotally that he employed TB patients in building miles of rock walls around his home with the valley's endless supply of rocks, presumably to foster physical fitness in the afflicted people. We also hear that he treated his patients with *Yerba santa*, an extremely common plant in our mountains that was used by the local Indians to strengthen the lungs. However, neither of these treatment stories can be verified.

Dr. Briggs didn't last too long himself, dying in 1893, probably from TB, perhaps complicated by the previously mentioned gunshot wound that never really healed. Although he was in the valley only twelve years, he had a huge impact on its development, one aspect of which was to make it a mecca for health seekers. Briggs's home, located up on Briggs Terrace just off Freeman near Terrace Drive, was bulldozed in the 1960s—nothing remains. Higher up at Freeman and Maurice is an old water tower that probably belonged to him as well. It has been converted to a cute little home but still retains the shape of the water tower. There is a photo of a decorative fountain, spraying high into the air, in Dr. Briggs's front yard. A water tower such as this would have provided enough water pressure for a fountain.

Farther down Briggs Terrace, just off Shields and about a half block up from Goss Canyon Drive, is the former location of Utley's Sanitarium.

Again, local lore has it that a couple of the houses in a little private cul-de-sac date back to the sanitarium, along with a few of the rock walls. I was contacted a couple years ago by someone in this neighborhood whose home was haunted by a very active ghost—not surprising given that patients in TB sanitariums checked in but rarely checked out.

Down the hill, on Foothill at the present-day site of Ralph's Supermarket, was Kimball Sanitarium, the most notorious of the local sanitariums. While the TB sanitariums made up the bulk of the facilities in the valley, Kimball was a sanitarium for the treatment of mental illness and drug and alcohol addiction. It was creepy looking, operating out of an old Victorian mansion with a cement blockhouse-style lockup facility to one side. It was completely demolished in the early '60s, when the shopping mall was built, and the ground it sat on was excavated to make a flat pad for the stores. Only a couple things remain of the place. There's a house on Raymond that was a residence for the nurses, as well as a house over near the La Crescenta Library that had been an outbuilding and was moved off the property during demolition. Also, neighbor Joe Rakasits notes that the palm trees on the lower side of the Mormon Church parking lot were part of the sanitarium's landscaping.

Heading west in the valley, we find Dunsmore Park, which was established in 1933 as Mount Lukens Sanitarium and later renamed Dunsmore Sanitarium. The community building there is part of the original facility, and old photos of the building show the high-peaked roof as having dormer windows, indicating that perhaps patients or staff slept upstairs. The artistic rock walls that run throughout the park were built by the owner and, perhaps, the patients of the sanitarium in the '40s and '50s. Glendale bought the sanitarium to convert into a park in 1957 and demolished a couple of the buildings but fortunately kept the main house and most of the imaginative rock walls for us to enjoy today.

Moving farther west, there was Hillcrest Sanitarium at the top of Lowell Avenue. During its forty-year run, Hillcrest treated a wide variety of illnesses, including mental illness, TB, senility and alcoholism. A housing development was built on its site, and no trace remains of this old sanitarium.

In addition to these large sanitariums were the small home-based sanitariums—houses converted into places where victims of a wide variety of afflictions could convalesce. For example, Perry Whiting, for whom the neighborhood of Whiting Woods is named, left behind a huge mansion when he moved from the valley. It was turned into a small sanitarium. There were also hotels and boardinghouses that catered to health seekers. The

Dunsmore Park was once Dunsmore Sanitarium, a tuberculosis sanitarium. In the late 1950s, the property was sold to the City of Glendale, and the sanitarium building was repurposed as a community building for Dunsmore Park. *Photo by Mike Lawler.*

La Crescenta Hotel, sometimes known as the Silver Tree Inn, at Foothill Boulevard and Rosemont was a grand three-story hotel that listed the clean, pure, health-giving qualities of the air in La Crescenta as one of its attractions. It ran from 1888 into the 1920s. A writer at the time described it as a "restful home-like retreat for the lone invalid seeking health among strange faces in our pure mountain air." The nearby but smaller Fairmont Hotel on Fairmont Avenue near Briggs was open during that same period and listed the same attractions for health seekers. Over on the La Cañada side, there was Verdugo Heights, run by Delia Dunks. It was situated on the north slope of the valley near where today's Angeles Crest Highway ends its long, straight uphill run and begins to curve up into the San Gabriel Mountains. Its advertising stated that its location was "particularly dry and healthful, free from fog, and is an excellent home for those afflicted with pulmonary difficulties." The health resort/boardinghouse existed from the early 1880s into the 1890s, but the structure lasted as a home in various remodeled forms all the way into the 1960s, when it was finally demolished.

Overall, the Crescenta Valley in its early years was a mecca for the infirm, and sanitariums and the pursuit of health can be counted as the first and founding industry of the community.

Hillcrest Sanitarium

Hillcrest Sanitarium was one of the larger sanitariums in the valley, housing from fifty up to nearly two hundred patients in several buildings between the late 1920s and the late 1960s. Although it started as a tubercular sanitarium, its staff treated a wide variety of chronic illnesses. In later years, it morphed into a home for the aged and, at one point near the end, a facility for alcoholics. Its most infamous years were during World War II, when it was taken over by the government to house hundreds of Japanese American internees that had contracted TB in the crowded internment camps.

It was located on a small plateau at the top of Lowell Avenue, what is today Markridge Estates. Lowell Avenue turns into Markridge at the very top. From there, if you turn left onto Skyridge Drive, you are more or less following the old driveway of the old sanitarium. An old topographical map shows fifteen separate buildings on the property, including two large patient facilities. The houses on Sky View Lane and Brittany Lane sit right where the sanitarium buildings were. Look out over the valley from here, and you'll see much the same view as thousands of patients at Hillcrest saw—and for hundreds of them, it was their last view of this world.

Crescenta Valley resident James Gerhard took an interest in Hillcrest Sanitarium, as he used to explore its ruins when he was a kid in the late 1970s and early '80s. He related that there were concrete slabs where the buildings had been and that as kids, they would occasionally camp out on the slabs. He said the overgrown remnants of the old landscaping, a proliferation of exotic plants, gave it a creepy quality that was irresistible to a young boy.

James purchased some postcards on eBay that show Hillcrest Sanitarium in its glory days. The landscaping is gorgeous, with eucalyptus and cypress trees scattered across a base of pampas grass and flowering plants around the buildings, all framing sweeping vistas of the valley and Los Angeles.

The Hillcrest Sanitarium, built in 1928 at the top of Lowell Avenue, was a high-end facility, as evidenced by this postcard. The sanitarium's advertising carried the tagline "Where health is in the air"—which was about all it had to offer tuberculosis patients of that era. *James Gerhard.*

This view of a building at the large Hillcrest Sanitarium shows that each room had a window facing out over what must have been a spectacular view of the valley and the Los Angeles Basin. *James Gerhard.*

One card shows the Trudeau Building and another card the Gould Building. Both have a center lobby with two long wings on each side. Each wing consists of connected cottages, each with its own picture window looking out over the gardens and the valley. The postcard carries the slogan "Hillcrest Sanitarium, Elevation 2,300 Feet—Where Health Is in the Air" and gives a phone number of Sunland 2277.

It must have been a high-class place in its early years. A *Los Angeles Times* article from 1932 describes its purchase by a new owner, a Dr. Coghlan, for $75,000, a phenomenal sum in the darkest years of the Great Depression. As stipulated in the deal, he was to put in another $100,000 in improvements to the nine-acre property. The article mentions that the sanitarium had been built four years earlier and that it had beds for fifty patients.

Part of the drawing power of the property was that film star Clara Bow had spent some well-publicized time at Hillcrest for "recuperation from the effects of a strenuous career." Bow was a silent film mega-star in the 1920s who mixed the glamour of Madonna with the out-of-control craziness of Lindsey Lohan. She was the inspiration for cartoon character Betty Boop and Peppy Miller, the female lead in the Academy Award–winning picture *The Artist*. She was unstable and was in and out of sanitariums for much of her career. The fact that she was at Hillcrest at the very height of her fame attests to its high-class status.

Hillcrest continued to operate as a high-end sanitarium through the '30s, and we found reference to another wealthy doctor, Austrian émigré Dr. Max Gecht, also owning it during that period. When World War II started, Hillcrest Sanitarium was taken over by the U.S. government, and a whole new chapter of misery opened for Hillcrest.

In 1942, the U.S. government set up ten relocation camps in the western United States, into which were crowded 120,000 U.S. citizens of Japanese descent. In conditions like that, disease was bound to spread, so the government requisitioned Hillcrest Sanitarium to treat TB patients from the internment camps. It was privately operated but administered by the county, and the patients were guarded by armed county sheriffs.

Several letters from internees treated at Hillcrest survive today, and they document a dismal existence. Following are segments of a letter from an artist, Ido Mita, to her friend and fellow artist Estelle Peck Ishigo. Estelle was a Caucasian woman married to a Japanese American man, and she voluntarily accompanied her husband to the Heart Mountain internment camp in Wyoming.

Hillcrest Sanitarium, La Crescenta, California, August 13, 1942

Dear Estelle, I came across your name in one of the copies of Pomona Center News that a patient here was reading. I hope this letter will reach you before you and Arthur leave for Wyoming.

I was "evacuated" to this sanatorium on May 8th. We are high in the foothills near Tujunga. This is a concentration point for Japanese tuberculars. There are about 160 of us here now. I never lived with so many Japanese in my life, let alone sick people. There are all sorts of people, young and old, well ones and some dying ones. In fact ,about seven of us have died since I came up here.

I am getting along OK, in spite of the fact that the food here is very, very bad, and not enough to keep a dog alive. All this is due to the fact that the place is privately owned, and is under contract with the County (the County in turn with the Army) to house and feed us. Every time we hear what "gochiso" [loosely translates to "feast"] *you people in different centers are eating, it certainly makes us envious.*

Please write and let me know when you get to Wyoming. I hope you have nice subjects to paint up there. I haven't been doing anything up here yet. The grounds are too artificially landscaped for me to paint. The hills are one of those rocky, spotty and ugly things that even the magic of light cannot improve.

—*Edo Mita*

I'm sure her view of our beautiful mountains was flavored by her sickness and her imprisoned state, but by Christmas of '43, she had sent Estelle a pretty hand-drawn Christmas card depicting the sanitarium framed by pines and the Crescenta Valley below, looking quite beautiful. Edo was still at Hillcrest into 1945.

In a biography written about another internee, George Yuzawa, we find this sad story:

George's younger sister, Chieko, 19 years old at the time of the evacuation, was not permitted to join her family at Santa Anita or Amache for health reasons. Shortly before the evacuation, Chieko contracted tuberculosis. The U.S. government moved her to Hillcrest Sanitarium, located in the mountains of northwest Los Angeles. She died there in 1942, never having seen her parents again. During her stay, George was given permission to leave the camp (with an army escort) only once to visit her. The second and final time he went was to claim her body.

We have no record of how many internees died at Hillcrest. It must have been a very sad place, and one surviving letter recounts one of the patients going insane. As the war wound down, Hillcrest returned to housing private patients.

When Glendale annexed a huge portion of the Crescenta Valley in the early '50s, businesses within the annexation had to apply for city permits. In 1951, Hillcrest Sanitarium was issued a twenty-five-year permit to operate a "home for the aged." However, by the mid-'60s, Hillcrest Sanitarium had gone out of business.

In 1967, the Milestone Foundation, based in Pasadena, applied with the City of Glendale to convert the empty facility into an alcoholic treatment hospital. The group was initially turned down by the city. The reasons given were that the property was zoned residential and that a center for treatment of alcoholics would be detrimental to the neighborhood. The city described the facility as dilapidated and said that the single road access to the sanitarium would be dangerous in a fire. Milestone Foundation argued that the twenty-five-year permit issued to Hillcrest was still in effect and that it had the legal right to operate a sanitarium, no matter what was being treated.

Milestone must have prevailed, as local lore tells us that it did indeed become a "dry-out" facility for alcoholics, operating under the name of the Pine Tree Lodge. Legend has it that drunks roamed the neighborhood, but that might just be gossip. Pine Tree Lodge couldn't have lasted very long and must have been demolished because by the early '70s, locals relate that there were only slabs where the buildings had been.

Longtime Crescenta Valley resident Karen Carlson wrote about her childhood memories of playing in the Hillcrest Sanitarium during the years it was temporarily abandoned (circa 1964–65) and before it was briefly reopened as the Pine Tree Lodge. Karen said that she and her best friend, Judy Thomsen, would push their bikes up the long hill to the dilapidated old sanitarium. She said they had the feeling then that the facility had been abandoned suddenly, as everything was still in place—washcloths hung over the edges of the tub, furniture and wheelchairs were ready for use and paperwork and case notes were strewn everywhere. The two girls found an old padded cell, and they played a dangerous game called "How Long Can You Stand to be Locked in the Cell?" One girl would enter the small, dark cell, while the other would hold the door shut. Karen said her friend Judy was a big strong girl and had the advantage. When Judy was locked inside, she was able to force the door open when she wanted out. Karen, on the other hand, was held in just a wee bit too long by the stronger Judy, and it was terrifying, which made it all the more fun.

While the athletic Judy occupied herself with riding the old wicker wheelchairs down the driveways and ravines, crashing into bushes and trees, the more academic Karen sat and read the patients' files. She became fascinated with one of the mental patients, a man she now calls "Mr. X." As she read his case files, she found herself rooting for his recovery and bemoaning his relapses. The experience profoundly affected her life. As an adult, she became a mental health professional, getting her masters degree in marriage and family counseling. And the athletic Judy? Well, of course, she became a PE teacher! Nearly fifty years later, they're still best friends and even work together in the Glendale school system—Ms. Thomsen as a physical education teacher and Ms. Carlson as a school counselor—perhaps due a little bit to their experiences at Hillcrest Sanitarium.

Warren Boehm, a longtime local insurance broker and former member of the Montrose Search and Rescue, gave me a few of his memories as well. His office was on Foothill at the bottom of Lowell, and he remembers well the public bus stopping there and herds of workers getting off to make the long hike up to Hillcrest. If they were headed up the hill when he was leaving his office, he'd give them a ride. Warren told me he was amazed at how beautiful it was at Hillcrest. There were big pine trees up there, and Warren says you felt like you were at Sequoia. They were all removed for the subdivision that is there today.

Warren also tells us that there was another sanitarium planned for that same area. In 1962, the old Le Mesnager Ranch, now Deukmejian Park, was being fought over by developers. One developer came in with a plan to build a one-hundred-bed sanitarium on a portion of the ranch between Dunsmore and Boston above Markridge. The plans didn't get much traction, as the residents up there fiercely fought the idea to a standstill.

In 1987, the drama of that piece of the valley began anew as a developer bought the Hillcrest property and proposed Markridge Estates, the development that is there today. The neighborhood below fought the development, and the Glendale planners sided with them. The developers appealed it all the way to a city council vote, where it was rejected again, based on fire and earthquake danger. Fire danger was a factor because there would be only one access road to the development, and the developers briefly proposed a bridge east across Cooks Canyon to connect to the top of Boston. Building bridges is a big deal, though, and the fire danger was mitigated with less cost by building a water tank above the development. Many locals remember it being painted by a local artist to look like a giant Coors can. Earthquake danger was, and still is, a factor at the development, as the Sierra Madre Fault runs through the valley just above Markridge. Eventually, the development was approved, and in the early '90s, the slabs from Hillcrest Sanitarium were bulldozed away and forty-two homes built.

On the Internet, Hillcrest Sanitarium comes up on a few "ghost hunter" websites, but I think that comes mainly from an old list of abandoned sanitariums that has been circulated by ghost hunters over the years rather than from any documented sightings of ghosts at the site.

James Gerhard was asked if he ever had any paranormal experiences when he was a kid exploring the ruins there in the '70s and '80s. He replied, "We never saw any ghosts up there, but I can tell you that there was a strange feeling I can't really describe. Maybe it was just the eerie surroundings, or maybe it was the spirits of those who passed away on that hill. I guess if ghosts exist, Hillcrest would be a prime place for them!" We'd have to ask the residents of Markridge Estates if they ever get any visits from the hundreds of patients that died in despair at Hillcrest Sanitarium.

KIMBALL SANITARIUM

Finding information on the local sanitariums has been difficult due to the ethics of patient confidentiality. A lot of what we know about Kimball Sanitarium is pieced together from random news clippings, eyewitness accounts from old-timers and some often-misleading Internet postings. Kimball Sanitarium is, without doubt, the most infamous of all the local sanitariums as it was a true and classic insane asylum. Adding to the creepy factor was its setting—it was based in an old Victorian mansion, with heavily wooded grounds making it invisible from the street.

The "Kimball" in Kimball Sanitarium was Merritt Kimball, a local boy raised in La Crescenta and married at St. Luke's. He and his brother Donald, who had lost a leg in France during World War I, seem to have been business partners in the sanitarium.

The Kimball boys had been raised in the mental health industry. Their father was Frederick Kimball, who was the first superintendent of Patton State Mental Hospital, which opened in San Bernardino in 1893. It was originally named the Highland Insane Asylum. The national attitude for treating the mentally ill at that time was shifting from community or family responsibility (i.e., "the crazy aunt locked in the attic") to the large hospital format that would ensure reasonably good treatment and provide some hope of recovery. The Highland Insane Asylum was the first mental hospital in Southern California and housed approximately one thousand male and female patients. This was before any aggressive treatments of mental illness had been developed, such as medication, shock treatment or lobotomies. The only treatment was rest and, of course, isolation from the larger society. For the patients, it was an "asylum" in the literal definition of the word—a place of refuge, a sanctuary.

Frederick Kimball retired from his position as head of the asylum in 1910, and sometime after this point, he moved to La Crescenta with his wife to raise his two boys. He opened his own sanitarium, Banksia Place, at 5227 Santa Monica Boulevard in Hollywood (the corner of Santa Monica and Kingsley). That site today is the Kingsley Elementary School.

Banksia Place appears to have been an upscale sort of sanitarium. An advertisement from that time described it as being devoted to the care and treatment of "the nervous." It further described the torments of those suffering from nervous exhaustion and how contact with the "strong and healthy" would only further wear down the spent nerves of Banksia Place's prospective patients. It invited the reader to "get away for awhile" in the distinctly un-institutional air of this sanitarium, with individual cottages and lush rose-covered gardens. According to the ad, prominent businessmen and professionals had taken advantage of the offer of the kind and intelligent ministrations of Mr. and Mrs. Kimball. It can be assumed as well that Banksia Place's Hollywood location gave Kimball a film industry connection, which perhaps later carried over to La Crescenta's Kimball Sanitarium being noted for its celebrity patients.

Frederick Kimball of Banksia Place and his son Merritt of Kimball Sanitarium were not doctors, as we would expect to find operating a mental health facility today. Nor was Agnes Richards of Rockhaven Sanitarium or Milton Hofert of Dunsmore Sanitarium. They were administrators there to "warehouse" the sick or insane, with little hope of any kind of medical cure and therefore no need for a medical degree. It can be argued that the popularity of brutal shock treatment and lobotomies, which did not require a doctor to perform, were due in part to the sanitarium owner's desires to do something—anything—to help their patients.

Young Merritt Kimball grew up around the mentally ill, and so it was perhaps natural that the La Crescenta resident would, in the local economic boom of the early '20s, look along Foothill Boulevard for a suitable property to start his own insane asylum.

KIMBALL SANITARIUM OPENS

Merritt decided to open a local mental sanitarium in partnership with his brother, Dr. Donald Kimball. Donald Kimball had lost a leg in France in World War II while serving as a motorcycle messenger. Near the front lines, motorcycle messengers would speed along the country roads at night with no lights on so as not to attract enemy fire. He had collided head-on with a truck, also driving with no lights. He nearly died and was lucky to get off with just an amputated leg. This accident had cut short his goal of completing his training in dentistry at USC. After a long recuperation, however, he did become a prominent doctor in La Cañada. And what better medical field than podiatry for a man with one leg?

Merritt and Donald had plenty of choices in the Crescenta Valley for their proposed sanitarium. In the early '20s, there were many large rambling estates left over from the 1880s, when La Crescenta had attracted wealthy residents looking for a healthy climate. The Kimballs chose for their sanitarium a ten-acre estate adjacent to the huge La Crescenta Hotel at Rosemont and Foothill. The estate had been built sometime in the 1880s, presumably for Father Queteaux, who had been a priest at San Juan Capistrano and a missionary in North Africa. That site today is the Ralph's and Rite-Aid on Foothill.

Most of what we know about the property comes from longtime residents Joe and Linda Rakasits, who today live nearly next door to where Kimball Sanitarium once was. Joe and his brothers had the demolition contract for the old sanitarium in the '60s, so Joe and Linda had spent some time exploring the abandoned asylum before it was torn down.

The Victorian house that was central to the sanitarium, as well as home to Merritt and his wife, was beautifully built. There was a full-width porch, and the front door opened onto a reception area, with a parlor and office beyond. Central in the living room was an ornate fireplace featuring ceramic tiles of classic Greek figures, all surrounded with intricately carved wood. The second story was accented with an octagonal tower with a big weathervane on top. Joe says there was extensive use of cherry wood throughout, in bookshelves and staircases, and that the level of craftsmanship was amazing. By the way, a gorgeous cherry wood staircase was pulled out of the old house and installed in a new home up near Pinecrest. Check your staircases, readers!

There was a big barn to the east, and behind the house were several small cottages with Murphy beds, presumably for patients who could be trusted. The main event, however, was the building to the west that had the padded cells. Joe describes it as a cement blockhouse, long and low. On one end was an open shower area. A very wide hallway ran the length, with padded cells on each side, complete with leather manacles.

Joe salvaged a few items from the sanitarium that were being thrown out, including one of Merritt Kimball's scrapbooks from the '20s and '30s, when his business was growing. It's a fascinating book, full of news clippings about incidents that touched on his sanitarium. Equally interesting is the book into which the clippings are pasted—an old patient logbook, complete with their names and a running account of their daily expenses.

THE LIVES OF PATIENTS

The following poem, presumably written by a patient at Kimball Sanitarium, was pasted into Merritt Kimball's scrapbook. It illustrates the hopelessness experienced by patients at Kimball Sanitarium:

Oh! You are here to stay as long as you should
If you do for freedom feel the move
To escape, there's no chance on the card,
For the doors are locked so carefully
And the windows with wire are barred.

You can search for a pass
To get through the glass,
But it's not worthwhile at least;
For being a human, you are too large
To get out, like any small beast.

When you ask why the wires on the window stand
You are told by a nurse with a look so bland
"It's to keep out the flies that bug us so,"
And you are green enough to think it is true,
But for the fact that you still do not know.
For the truth is this, from one that is wise;
Their purpose you really can judge from their size.
While the flies they do keep out very well,
It's the bugs inside that they restrain.

R.E.D. June 9, 1927

Unfortunately, it was easy to have anyone of a disagreeable nature committed in the '20s and '30s. It can be gleaned from reading the history of mental institutions of that period that people were committed for mild retardation, alcoholism, homosexuality or just being plain weird. If someone was willing to pay your hospital bill, you could easily be locked up for a very long time. In Mr. Kimball's scrapbook, there is a newspaper clipping with the headline "Millionaire Says Wife Used Rum." The story outlines an ugly divorce case, during which the husband has his wife, who is in the midst of suing for divorce, arrested and held in a sanitarium (Kimball perhaps?) for several weeks for "using alcohol and other stimulants to excess." The legal system enjoyed free rein in committing citizens to institutions. In the 2008 film *The Changeling*, based on the true story of the 1920s Wineville Chicken Coop Murders, the LAPD has a woman committed to an insane asylum to silence her when she disputes their handling of the kidnapping of her son. Several patients at Kimball likely experienced the similar fate of being "put away" without legitimate cause.

There was no real treatment for mental illness at that time, so Kimball essentially served as a "holding station." The violent patients were locked inside padded cells and were restrained with manacles or in straitjackets. Nonviolent patients were allowed out onto the lush grounds of the sanitarium. There was no fence, so escapes did happen. A clipping in Kimball's scrapbook from 1929 titled "Police Hunt Missing Sanitarium Patient" shows that sometimes they just disappeared into the surrounding neighborhood. One local resident relates that in the '40s, as her family drove down Foothill past Kimball, several patients ran out into the street and tried unsuccessfully to commandeer their car. Her dad hit the accelerator and got away.

Running a sanitarium could be dangerous. Kimball's scrapbook is filled with news clippings of violent patients attacking their keepers: "Doctor Found Shot to Death at Sanitarium," "Woman Patient Arrested in Wounding of Psychiatrist," "L.A. Physician Shot Down by Woman Patient." These must have played on Merritt Kimball's mind, as we find later in the scrapbook his license to carry a concealed firearm, a .32 Colt pistol.

THE ANTI-SANITARIUM MOVEMENT

There's no arguing that Kimball Sanitarium had an ugly side and that the community was not thrilled with its presence or the presence of other sanitariums. During the 1920s, there was a housing boom, and new homeowners were naturally shy of building next to insane asylums or hospitals for those with tuberculosis, at that time an incurable infectious disease. Real estate interests and sanitariums began to find themselves at odds. Residents began showing up at permit application hearings for new sanitariums, and in October 1928, a permit for a new sanitarium, to be located just across the street from Kimball, was denied based on the objections of locals.

Tension came to a head in November 1928, when Agnes Richards, owner of Rockhaven, applied to the county to expand her sanitarium. Several local activists showed up at the county board of supervisors meeting to testify against Rockhaven's expansion. Amongst the valid objections were some wild accusations. One resident claimed that the presence of mental patients at Rockhaven was devaluing his property on Briggs above Foothill, several miles away. Another testified that "wild-looking men" peering out through the fence of Rockhaven had been scaring neighbors (Rockhaven was a female-only facility). A former cook at Rockhaven testified that a patient there had poisoned the food of other patients. The board of supervisors issued a "stop-work order" for Rockhaven, and the county' public welfare committee was ordered to investigate.

Local activists kept up the pressure by immediately calling a couple mass meetings. They were well attended, with realtors and prominent families weighing in, calling for a total ban on sanitariums and establishing a fund to threaten legal action against the owners. It was proposed that meetings be held with the sanitarium owners to formally ask them to move out of the area. Even the local chamber of commerce was flirting with condemning the

LA CRESCENTA, CALIFORNIA

center over which one may travel from one end of the state to the other.

Considerable street work already has been done and more improvements are contemplated in the near future. One noteworthy improvement now under way is the new 100-foot Foothill boulevard from the City of Pasadena on the east, to the westerly limits of La Crescenta, skirting the southern base of the Sierra Madre mountains.

Motor Traffic

Fifteen thousand automobiles were shown by official count to have passed through La Crescenta Sunday, January 22, 1928, between the hours of 8 a. m. and 8 p. m.

Bank

THE FIRST NATIONAL BANK OF LA CRESCENTA was established in 1927.

Distance

La Crescenta is 14 miles from the center of Los Angeles.

It is within 35 minutes of the center of the metropolis by automobile, traveling over paved highways and about 45 minutes by electric car or stage line.

Rose Parade

It is about 15 minutes drive to the world-famous Tournament of Roses at Pasadena and also the famous Busch gardens, and Brookside Park.

Close To Beaches

It is about one hour's drive by automobile to the ocean beaches.

Location

Beautiful La Crescenta nestles on a gentle foothill slope of the Sierra Madre Mountains, and offers to those desiring a home, a location removed from the congestion of the city, yet near enough to enjoy all the advantages and privileges of the metropolis.

—3—

In the late 1920s, the La Crescenta Chamber of Commerce put out this brochure extolling the merits of the Crescenta Valley for businesses. Kimball Sanitarium is featured on page two, indicating the prominent role it and other sanitariums played in the business of the valley. *Glendale Public Library.*

sanitariums. Out of these meetings was formed the La Crescenta Protective Association. There were several prominent locals on the group's board of directors, and its stated goal was to get rid of sanitariums.

Unfortunately for the credibility of the protective association, there was a faction that was still throwing out wild accusations. A speaker claimed that Rockhaven had, instead of the thirty female patients stated by Agnes Richards, upward of sixty male and female patients, and a former employee told the crowd that Agnes Richards had been drunk most of the time she worked there. Agnes Richards fought back hard with a $200,000 slander suit against two of the speakers, one of which she won several months later. The county public welfare committee brought back a report that the accusations made against Rockhaven were false. Crescenta Valley was deeply divided.

We know from looking at Merritt Kimball's preserved personal scrapbook that he was watching all this closely. Every news article about the Rockhaven fight is carefully dated and pasted in the scrapbook. He must have known that he would be targeted next if the anti-sanitarium forces gained ground. Looking at the scrapbooks entries, we see that at this juncture, Kimball began to get involved in local service groups. He threw himself fully into the task of becoming a community leader. Perhaps he saw this as his business's salvation, or maybe he simply wanted to give back to the community. Whatever the case, by the early '30s, he had leadership roles in the Red Cross, the Masons, the Crescenta Valley Chamber of Commerce, the Verdugo Hills Merchants Association, the Foothill Boulevard Association, the Disaster Relief Corporation and the American Legion. In 1935, he was elected to the Glendale Board of Education, on which he served for over a decade.

We never heard from the La Crescenta Protective League again, and formal opposition to the sanitariums died out. In 1933, Merritt Kimball opened a second sanitarium, Mount Lukens Sanitarium (later Dunsmore Sanitarium, now Dunsmore Park) with no opposition. We'll never really know his initial motivation for becoming involved in community leadership, but it's obvious that by the late '30s, he was fully engaged in making our community a better place. Although his sanitarium was not popular locally, he had become a true community and business leader.

HOLLYWOOD STARS

As stated before, patient confidentiality hinders our knowledge of the identities of patients at Kimball. We have some pretty murky local lore referring to Kimball as being the "Screen Actor's Hospital," even though the actual Motion Picture and Television Hospital has existed in Woodland Hills since 1942. Perhaps Kimball subcontracted with them due to the overload of mental illness in the movie industry?

One local legend states that actor Bela Lugosi had been treated for his famous morphine addiction at Kimball, very unflatteringly portrayed in the movie *Ed Wood.* History says that Lugosi suffered chronic intense pain from injuries he received in World War I service. After years of being prescribed morphine-based painkillers, he attempted to break his addiction and in 1955 had himself committed to the state hospital in Norwalk. A couple unreliable Internet sources say that he initially received treatment at the Motion Picture Hospital and was later transferred to Norwalk. However, the website of the Motion Picture Hospital doesn't list him as having been a patient. A former nurse at Kimball, a Mrs. Chatterton, clearly remembered Lugosi being at Kimball for a short time. She vividly remembers him being very grumpy, as he naturally would be during drug withdrawal.

Another star who spent time at Kimball is Frances Farmer. Farmer had a meteoric career in film and stage starting in the '30s and ending spectacularly during WWII. She had always been strong willed and outspoken, and as alcoholism crept into her life, she began to have problems with the law. She was ticketed for driving with her lights on in a World War II blackout zone in Santa Monica. She failed to pay the fines, and an arrest warrant was issued. Picked up by the police at the Knickerbocker Hotel in Hollywood, she initiated a spectacular knockdown brawl, which escalated the next morning at her hearing. After throwing an inkwell at the judge and knocking down a couple policemen, she was sentenced to 180 days in jail. As they carried her away, she was screaming, "Have you ever had a broken heart?!"

Farmer's family was able to get her transferred to the psych ward at County General and, later, Kimball Sanitarium. Frances spent nine months at Kimball. Her attending psychiatrist diagnosed her as paranoid schizophrenic and prescribed insulin shock therapy, a common treatment for schizophrenia in the '40s and '50s. Insulin shock therapy was labor intensive and required a highly trained staff. The patient was given injections of 100 to 150 units of insulin, and sometimes as high as 450 units. The patients often convulsed during and after the treatments. We see a graphic portrayal of Frances Farmer having a seizure during treatment at Kimball in the movie *Frances*, starring Jessica Lange. Sometimes electroshock therapy would be included in these sessions. A coma lasting an hour or so would be ended with a dose of intravenous glucose. This went on every day for several months. Patients were typically nauseous, sweaty and restless between treatments.

After nine months of this, Frances Farmer escaped from the minimum-security Kimball Sanitarium. She walked twenty miles to her half-sister's house, where her mother gained custody of her and moved her to Seattle. There she was again committed to the Western State Hospital. That hospital was, according to Frances Farmer's autobiography, a brutal prison where rapes and abuse were common. She probably wished she hadn't walked away from Kimball!

After a couple years there, she was released and began to rebuild her life, even enjoying a comeback in the '50s and '60s. She had most likely been nothing more than an alcoholic yet had spent years in insane asylums. Farmer's shocking story, played out in part right here in La Crescenta, was an indictment of the mental health system at that period, when nearly anyone could be declared insane.

KIMBALL SANITARIUM BECOMES RALPH'S SUPERMARKET

By the late '50s, it appeared that Merritt Kimball, owner/operator of Kimball Sanitarium, was ready to get out of the sanitarium business. A full-size community hospital was being planned for the growing Crescenta Valley, and Merritt Kimball had put his property at Rosemont and Foothill in the running as a potential site. Several news articles in 1958 detailed the competition between three local hospital proposals. Kimball had teamed with a developer who was proposing a fifty-four-bed hospital of almost twenty-two thousand square feet on the Kimball site. He was competing against Sidney Brittain, who had planned the Foothill Valley Hospital on the east side of Sparr Heights. The third competitor was J. Morgan Greene, who proposed an unnamed hospital on his property on or around the Indian Springs swimming pool.

Oddly, the city of Glendale was less than enthusiastic about another hospital, stating it had enough already, and even turned down the initial applications for both the Sparr Heights location and the Indian Springs location. The Kimball property, outside Glendale city limits, seemed a shoo-in for the valley's first hospital, and the *Los Angeles Times* even declared that the new hospital at Rosemont and Foothill would break ground in November of '58. But as we all know, things changed, and J. Morgan Greene got the upper hand with his Indian Springs property. Starting in the early '60s, Greene developed property higher up on the hill for the hospital and used the excavated dirt from that site to fill in the Indian Springs pool and canyon. He built a shopping center there and moved the old Behrens Hospital from Glendale up to his new site to open as Verdugo Hills Hospital in 1972.

This left Merritt Kimball looking for a new plan for his old sanitarium site. He leased his property to a development firm in 1961, and by '62, plans were rolling for a big shopping center. After four decades, Kimball Sanitarium was closing. Joe Kroening of Andy's Transfer helped the Kimballs move out, and he had some sad memories of the event:

> *As I recall, there were quite a number of "little cottages" on the property. Merritt Kimball said, "Just follow Mrs. Kimball around, and she will show what to take," and we did just that. As I recall, we moved what they were saving up to a house—I believe theirs—on Briggs Avenue north of the sanitarium. The "little cottages" were inhabited by one, two or three men. Most were veterans of World War I and World War II. They were pretty well terrified, as it seemed they had been living at Kimball's since they left the service. I can still recall some of them clinging to Mrs. Kimball crying that they "did not want to leave and what would they do?" It was sad then, and it's sad now. I guess post-traumatic stress disorder was as common then as it is now for our returning vets.*

The acres of avocado trees and pine trees were cut down, and the eleven-room Victorian mansion and elaborate carriage house were demolished. The old three-story La Crescenta Hotel went down at the same time. Joe Rakasits, whose brother had the demolition contract, culled a few gems out of the trash cans, including Merritt Kimball's scrapbook, from which much of our knowledge of Kimball Sanitarium comes from today. Tons of earth were moved to make the pad flat. The shopping center went up quickly, with the main stores being, west to east, Builder's Emporium (today Ralph's), Food Giant (soon replaced by Alpha Beta), Nahas department store and Thrifty Drug Store, with a number of small stores on the east side, including a childhood favorite of many adults today, John Henry's Ice Cream Parlor. A few years ago, Builder's Emporium and Alpha Beta closed, and their buildings were joined together to create a giant Ralph's, where locals shop today. For your shopping enjoyment: the Kimballs' offices and residence were located where the liquor department is now, the cottages for the nonviolent patients were in the dairy section and the padded cells would have been in the bakery.

We don't know what happened to the Kimballs. They were doing a difficult, unpopular and, sometimes, dangerous job with the best medical knowledge of the day. They were good people, community leaders who were serving a segment of society most of us would rather ignore. They did their best to make our world a better place.

About the Authors

Gary Keyes taught history, government and sociology at Crescenta Valley High School in La Crescenta for thirty-nine years. Currently, he is an adjunct professor of social science at Glendale Community College in Glendale, California. As a resident of the foothill communities for the past forty-five years, he became interested in local history when he helped members of his son's Boy Scout troop obtain their Citizenship in the Community badges. Today, he lives in La Cañada with a very supportive wife of forty-nine years.

Mike Lawler was born with a passion for history and spent much of his childhood digging holes in his yard in La Crescenta, looking for clues to the area's history. As a teenager, he was a student of Gary Keyes and was fascinated with Keyes's focus on some of the darker aspects of history. As an adult, he became a community leader in bringing local history to life with the Historical Society of the Crescenta Valley. He was thrilled to once again team up with Keyes to air Crescenta Valley's "dirty laundry."